The
MISMATCHED
HUMAN

OUR FIGHT FOR A
MEANINGFUL EXISTENCE

MARK A. HAWKINS

Cold
Noodle
Creative

Cold
Noodle
Creative

Mark A. Hawkins

The Mismatched Human

Cold Noodle Creative

Softcover ISBN 978-1-7782546-0-4
Electronic ISBN 978-1-7782546-1-1

Cover & Text Design | Kristy Twellmann Hill
Art Direction | Fleck Creative Studio

For Yoona.

The **MISMATCHED HUMAN**

PREFACE

"I don't even know why I'm alive anymore," she finally cried after unsuccessfully holding back tears. Maddie had come to my high school counselling office at eleven in the morning, red-faced and upset. She sobbed for several more minutes before reaching the point when she could breathe normally again. As a high school counsellor, I would usually ask what happened to make her feel this way, but for some reason that just did not feel right to me in the moment. So, I went with my gut, and in a very surprised and curious tone I asked, "Oh, you knew why you were alive before?"

The question took her totally off guard. No one had ever asked her such a thing. Thoroughly stunned, she stopped crying and looked up at me like I was crazy. After a long silence and with furled eyebrows, she finally replied, "Wait... aren't I supposed to know why I'm alive?"

"Well, I sure as hell don't," I said.

She cracked a tiny smile and what followed was not a conversation about tests, post-secondary, or her parents' expectations, but about how having a full-blown crisis of meaning has become the new normal for being human.

She had come into my office thinking there was something wrong with her for "losing" purpose in her life, but there was nothing wrong with her at all. Instead, it was the fact that the world today is increasingly mismatched and out of sync with the human desire for meaning. We must *fight* for our meaning and purpose now, but before we can do that, we must first learn how this mismatch came to be.

INTRODUCTION

How should we measure the success of a species? If it is by sheer numbers, then humans are a very successful species indeed. However, if we measure it by wellbeing and life satisfaction then our success is very much in question, especially when so many of us are struggling with very preventable mental health issues. Much of this is because modern humans are suffering from a crisis of meaning that may be the root cause of many of our personal and global problems today.

There are so many of us just walking around feeling half alive and going through psychological and emotional pain that one cannot help but think that there must be something fundamentally wrong with the way we are living and the way our society has become.

MEANING IS ESSENTIAL FOR HUMANS

Meaning is becoming harder for us to maintain at a time when we need it more than ever. According to the Canadian Mental Health Association, in any given year, 1 in 5 people in Canada will experience a mental health problem or illness, and by age 40, about 50% of the population will have had a mental illness.[1] The pace of life, the demands of technology, and the sheer complexity of our world make it more difficult for us to focus on finding our purpose. One thing I will say with certainty is that in today's world when our lives can be so confusing and chaotic, the importance of having meaning and purpose cannot be understated. But our need for a meaningful existence is not new by any stretch of the imagination. It is essential for our mental health and always has been.

Friedrich Nietzsche, the nineteenth-century philosopher, stated that a person who has a *why* to live for can bear almost any *how*. Irvin Yalom, one of the greatest American psychiatrists, argues that meaning in life is one of the only ways to ease the anxiety that many of us suffer from daily, and it is by finding meaning in life that an individual can cope with their finitude.[2] Viktor Frankl, the famous psychiatrist who lived through the concentration camps of Auschwitz and Dachau, wrote that those prisoners who were most likely to survive were oriented towards a future meaning that they wanted to fulfill. Similarly, he says that all of our mental health depends on "the striving and struggling for something worth longing for and groping for."[3] With all his knowledge and experience, Frankl concludes that having meaning to one's existence can sustain a person even in the most extreme circumstances. Consequently, a focus on the discovery and creation of meaning in our lives is likely to alleviate many of the issues that bring us to counselling therapy.[4]

On the other hand, a lack of meaning seems to do the exact opposite, causing mental illness and life dissatisfaction. Carl Jung wrote that the absence of meaning in life plays a crucial role in the development of mental illness.[5] Likewise, Yalom says that a sense of meaninglessness is associated with psychopathology in a roughly linear sense, which means that the less personal meaning we experience, the greater the severity of our psychopathology.[6]

Not only is meaning something that helps us to cope with the inevitable suffering that life brings and prevents mental illness, but it is also necessary for life satisfaction. This is why Frankl says that besides basic physical survival, it is meaning that humans need most for mental health. Today, we see that a lack of meaning makes it difficult for us to wake up and cope with our day-to-day life. For many of us, at some point in our lives, we realize that our work needs to have a meaningful purpose besides making money.

While many people today and throughout history have found meaning through organized religion, there is a large segment of the world's population that is either atheist or agnostic. These people do not necessarily deny that there is some sort of god or meaning to our lives and universe, but question whether humans can ever know for sure. For these people, the meaning that religion provides is dubious. Even those who are members of an organized religion often have trouble sustaining meaning in their lives because there are just so many perplexing aspects of life with which even religious folks struggle. So, even for those of us who are devout in our religious practice, meaning is still something that can falter.

THE EXISTENTIAL CRISIS: WHAT IS LIFE ABOUT ANYWAY?

A crisis of meaning, or what is sometimes called an existential crisis, is when we begin to question what life is all about. These crises come in all shapes and sizes. There is the "dark night of the soul," which religious folklore describe as when one who is destined to become a great spiritual leader begins to question their faith. Or there is the midlife crisis in which we question the path we took in the first half of our lives. There is even the high school graduate paralyzed with fear over their future. Then there is everything in between. It happens whenever we begin to question what our purpose is and what we should do with our time on this planet. People of modern industrialized nations, and I would argue humans in general, are not content with just living in and of itself. We need a grander reason for it.

We are not always aware that we are experiencing an existential crisis either. They can show up as anxiety, depression, addiction, insomnia, and many other psychological or physical symptoms that we either rationalize as just part of modern life or that we try to numb by popping a pill. But these band-aid solutions, while having their place, will not take the place of having a clear sense of purpose. While the crisis of meaning may be something we think is reserved for a small emotional and depressive segment of industrialized society, it is actually an integral part of being human. In fact, Jesus, Mohammad, and Siddhartha Gautama (Buddha) all questioned the nature of existence before coming to their various conclusions about life.

At some point in our lives, we will experience a crisis of meaning to some degree. Something about life in modern society is making them more prevalent than ever before. It is undeniable that having meaning is one of the most important aspects of living a fulfilling and satisfying life, yet why we need meaning, why it is difficult to sustain, and why crises of meaning became so commonplace are the focus of this book.

WHAT THIS BOOK IS ABOUT

On any bookshelf in a bookstore or online, we will see dozens of books promising "the answer" by the end of reading it. Modern self-help gurus promise that if we do enough inner work, we will discover a place deep inside of us that whispers our true purpose on this planet. This is not one of those books. There are no quick fixes or straight paths to personal meaning, but I hope this book will help the reader gain a new understanding of humanity's struggle for meaning and purpose.

As such, this book takes a historical or genealogical perspective by tracking how we have ended up where we are today and how the human experience of meaning and purpose has transformed over time. It traces how major shifts in human history have created a mismatch between our psychophysical (psychological and biological) nature and our current environment.

This book will look at how and why this mismatch came to be and how our attempts to overcome this mismatch have made it worse. It will give the reader a fighting chance to live more meaningfully by understanding these shifts and how they affect our experience of meaning and purpose. We will explore why we seem to need meaning as much as we need air or food, and how we got to a point in our history when many of us are miserable and crises of meaning are routine. It is more important than ever for our collective wellbeing that we learn the history of meaning. Only then can we change the narratives around crises of meaning to ones largely a result of our culture, society, and historical context rather than as problems that come from within those suffering from them. Finally, this book is an account of how we have reached such a crisis point of meaning and mental health. While I hope the account itself helps in lessening these crises in our lives, if we can shine some light on some of the problematic narratives that have developed as a result of our mismatch, we may be able to find sustainable meaning in our modern world.

"The heavens themselves run continuously around, the sun riseth and sets, the moon increaseth and decreaseth, stars and planets keep their constant motions, the air is still tossed by the winds, the waters ebb and flow, to their conservation no doubt, to teach us that we should ever be in action."[7]

— *Robert Burton*, The Anatomy of Melancholy

Chapter 1
WHAT IS MEANING?

MOVEMENT: THE FUNDAMENTAL FORCE OF LIFE

Understanding how we have reached a state of existential crisis requires that we first understand the nature of what drives humans. To do this, we must start at the very beginning with a force so obvious that many of us have completely overlooked it —movement.

Almost all spiritual and philosophical disciplines have acknowledged that movement, flux, and change are principal forces that permeate our entire existence. This is succinctly stated by twentieth-century social psychologist Erich Fromm when he says there is "only one crucial point: the concept of process, activity, and movement as [an essential] element of being."[8]

Movement was considered so important to Greek philosophers that what they called the Unmoved Mover was the fundamental cosmic force in the universe or God.[9] This Unmoved Mover can be thought of as a state of eternal unhindered enjoyable activity that moves us toward fulfillment, which is the natural inclination of our soul.[10] In fact, many Greek philosophers considered the study of movement in the cosmos to be the most important task of the philosopher.

In Taoism, the *Tao* is thought to be the patterns that keep the universe in balance. Alan Watts describes the Tao in terms of movement: "It has the sense of rhythmic motion, of going on and stopping… and so you get the idea of a sort of rhythmic intelligence that ebbs and flows like the tides."[11]

Similarly, movement is seen as a primary, universal force in Hinduism and Buddhism as well. The word *Samsara,* which refers to the state of life in the world, is derived from the Sanskrit word for "wandering." Samsara is rooted in the term *Samsr,* which means to go round, revolve, pass through a succession of states, to go towards or obtain.[12] Sarvepalli Rashakrishnan, the philosopher and second president of India, describes Buddhist philosophy as follows: "Impressed by the transitoriness of objects, the ceaseless mutation and transformation of things, Buddha formulated a philosophy of change. He reduces… things to forces, movements, sequence, and processes and develops a dynamic conception of reality…there is no entity that can endure its own being without change."[13]

Carl Jung referred to movement as the *anima* archetype, from the Latin meaning "the animating principle" that gives something its soul or life. It is also translated as breath and spirit. It is the force that animates or moves all things in the universe. Jung argued that this archetype manifested itself in the stories, folklore, and myths of all cultures as well as in our individual dreams.[14]

From the 1920s, theories in astrophysics have corroborated that the universe, as we know it, is expanding. This implies that matter expands outward from some origin we have not yet located.

When we look into phenomenology and hermeneutics, the idea of self-movement is the main thrust of Martin Heidegger's seminal work *Being and Time*, in which he theorizes that the nature of being and existence is time, and that time, at least for us humans, is movement.[15] Thus, movement is a primordial force that we all experience and that presents itself in numerous ways.

If movement and dynamism are foundational to life, we must inevitably ask, "What moves humans?"

OUR FUNDAMENTAL NEED FOR PLEASURE

Humans, just like all living things on Earth, are driven to survive. The universe in its great wisdom has ensured that the things necessary for our survival are also very pleasurable to us. So, it is, first and foremost, the pursuit of pleasure that moves humans. However, for today's humans, what we find pleasurable can be complicated.

In his book *The Birth and Death of Meaning*, Ernest Becker invites readers to repeat the phrase "humans are animals" a few times. Humans are animals, humans are animals, humans are animals. A bit dramatic? Perhaps. But Becker is trying to emphasize just how difficult it is for us to accept this concept. Try it yourself. Does this statement sit well with you? For many of us, the idea that we are merely animals is uncomfortable and maybe even disturbing. However, Becker's message is not that we are no different from animals, but that our behaviour can largely be explained by drives and instincts that are similar to animals. Namely, *survival*.

All living beings have an internal guidance system designed to help them survive. This system guides us to seek pleasure and avoid pain to maximize our chances of survival in the natural environment in which we first began to develop.

Is pleasure all there is, though? Humans exist for something more meaningful, don't we? Of course, but before we explore other aspects of our existence, we do need to accept that there is a deep, unavoidable part of us that does seek pleasure alone.

Roman philosopher Cicero, who was an adherent of the Stoic school of philosophy, wrote that the minute an animal (including a human) is born, its ultimate goal and chief good is seeking pleasure while pain and discomfort is the chief evil. Cicero views this aspect of behaviour as uncorrupted, pure, and whole.[16]

This was also the central view of one of the largest ancient Greek schools of philosophy, the Epicureans, who built almost their entire philosophy around the idea that pleasure is the highest good. An important distinction that the Epicureans make is between what they call *kinesthetic* pleasures and *katastematic* pleasures.

Kinesthetic pleasures are those pleasures that result from doing things—kinesthetic means movement. This refers to pleasure derived from either physical or mental movement.[17] Some examples would include sports, reading, and socializing.

On the other hand, katastematic pleasure makes us feel at peace with "what is." It is peace of mind and tranquility in the moment when we do not experience a single iota of pain or suffering.[18] In these moments, there is nothing more that we want or need. There is no yearning. It is that moment when you feel perfectly content after a satisfying meal. It is in the moments just after sex. It is when you are half-awake in the morning and the bed is perfectly comfortable.

More recently, Sigmund Freud came up with what he called the *will to pleasure,* the theory that "all facets of psychic life are constituted by the pursuit of greater pleasurable states or, synonymously, the reduction of unpleasant ones."[19] In other words, he believed that an important way that people try to achieve pleasure is by avoiding the feeling of instability that comes with psychological unrest. So humans and other animals try to achieve the most pleasurable state by either increasing pleasure or reducing pain.

WE DON'T LIKE PAIN

Avoiding pain is an equal and, in some cases, more powerful drive for humans than seeking pleasure. Not only do we have a natural fear of heights and loud noises, but our animal brains also have the fight, flight, and freeze responses to protect us from danger. In many cases, we will forgo what is pleasurable if we think it will be too painful to attain. Also, the relief of pain is experienced as pleasure while the end of a pleasurable activity is experienced as pain. For example, after a stressful day at work, even a dull evening at home is a great pleasure while returning to that same home after a fun vacation is often painfully boring. The Epicureans knew that overindulging in *vain pleasures* would eventually lead to more pain. Eating an indulgent meal now and then may be pleasurable but if we do it too much, we may end up overweight and feeling ill. So, we are left with managing a constant balance between pleasure and pain so we can continue to experience pleasure. Thus, rather than our behaviour being motivated by seeking pleasure alone, pleasure and pain are two sides of the same coin.

However, this constant balancing act is not just about physical pain or pleasure. When we feel like we have not lived up to our parent's expectations, when we experience anxiety about the future, or when our self-esteem is negatively affected by scrolling on social media, we are not feeling physical pain, but we are feeling psychological pain. Psychological pain may often be more distressing and prevalent than physical pain and have a more profound effect on our daily lives. This type of pain or pleasure does not come from the physical world but from the world created and conditioned into us through family, culture, and society that is often referred to as the symbolic world (which we will explore more later). The balancing of symbolic pleasure and pain in a symbolic world can be seen to drive most of our behaviours today and explain why we think we are more than mere animals seeking pleasure and recoiling from pain.

WE SEEK NEW AND EXCITING EXPERIENCES

While we find a range of things pleasurable, there are specific things that our minds and bodies crave because they are necessary for survival. The obvious ones are food and sex, and it may be that everything we do is related to increasing our ability to obtain these things. That is, it may be that other pleasures we seek are directly or indirectly connected to guaranteeing our survival. In particular, two of these other very powerful pleasures are excitement and novelty.

Bertrand Russell, a British philosopher from Cambridge, argues that excitement and novelty are some of the greatest pleasures for humans. Russell argues that seeking exciting or thrilling things is one of the main drivers of human behaviour.[20] It is not certain why we find excitement and novelty so pleasurable, but it is most likely related to survival and our need to seek new and better ways to survive, such as new sources of food.

Our need for movement and change is fundamental. Nothing makes this more obvious than the immense discomfort we feel when we are bored. In my first book, *The Power of Boredom*, I found that the pain of boredom itself is a powerful driver that makes us psychologically and physically move.

Many of us fantasize about a life of leisure, lying on the beach with no responsibilities. For many of us who live in a modern industrialized society that has created a lifestyle of chronic burnout and stress, it is only natural that we yearn for some mental and physical rest. And so it is no surprise that our fantasy is to live a life of complete leisure. We believe having nothing to strive for will bring us complete contentment. We are tired of striving so much. But have you seen what happens to people who have the time and means to live this kind of lifestyle? From my experience, a deep unsettling emptiness starts to creep in, and they actually begin to seek new challenges, experiences, and things to keep their minds interested. This is what Viktor Frankl referred to as the "Sunday neurosis," a phenomenon characterized by anxiety and restlessness because we cannot find anything worthwhile to do with our leisure time.

It can be expressed in many ways: going back to work, picking fights or starting arguments out of nowhere, obsessing over a project, or even making a radical change in life. How long can we go without having something to pursue? How long after starting retirement will the lack of purposeful direction become unbearable? Having nothing meaningful to do is one of the most painful things that humans experience and try to avoid.

WE NEED TO KEEP MOVING

Our need for engaging activity is such an integral part of our existence that Blaise Pascal, the French philosopher and mathematician, wrote that "[Humans] find nothing so intolerable as to be in a state of complete rest, without passions, without occupation, without diversion, [or] effort."[21] Despite some well-intentioned folks insisting that we have the ability to and will benefit from "emptying our minds," we love feeling engrossed, immersed, occupied, focused, in the flow, in the zone, and tuned in. Ironically, even when we practice emptying our minds to reach a more peaceful state, we are actively occupied in a purposeful pursuit! This is why Irvin Yalom writes that to find meaning in our lives we "must embrace the solution of engagement…and immerse oneself in the river of life and let the question [of meaning and purpose] drift away."[22] As important as meaning and purpose are to us, we cannot gain them by chasing after them directly. To quote Morris Berman, "the going is the goal."[23] Frankl states that rather than discovering or creating meaning by focusing on it, it must be pursued obliquely or indirectly through movement. So, what we seem to need is to feel engaged in some sort of forward movement in life.

WE LIKE COMMUNITY

In addition to finding pleasure in novelty and excitement, humans also enjoy being a part of a community of like-minded others with a common goal or purpose. This is because we need each other to survive. From our hunter-gatherer origins when we needed to cooperate to take down a mammoth, to today's urban environment where we are extremely interconnected at both the digital and physical levels, we are genetically programmed to want to be with each other. That is, while we have our personal views and preferences, life often feels more satisfying when our meaning is somehow tied to a group with which we feel comfortable.

Monasteries are excellent examples of humans' need for community. While the journey of enlightenment and religious study can be solitary, monks live together and support each other in their spiritual goals. While there are certainly stories of great religious figures who have gone it alone, most often these stories are more fiction than fact. It is difficult to go it alone at anything. Almost every ancient Greek school of philosophy insists that friendship and community are some of the highest goods.

THE PROBLEM: PLEASURES ARE FLEETING
Alas, all the moments of pleasure we derive from movement, community, excitement, food, or sex do not last forever. Boredom and negative thoughts begin entering our minds, or the longing for more fun, excitement, or connectedness makes us chase something that is not happening at the moment. Even in the middle of

a pleasurable activity, we know that it will not last forever. We chase pleasure over and over.

For most living beings on this planet, seeking pleasure and avoiding pain is the mechanism that is necessary for survival. However, because as humans we can reflect on our experience, we know that even if we feel pleasure now, it will not last forever. We can also imagine pleasurable experiences even if they are not happening at the moment and so we experience pain in the absence of the pleasure we imagine but are not currently experiencing. Think about it, our imaginations are continuously taking us to the next best possible reality. We may cognitively know that our home, relationships, and job are satisfactory, but we cannot help but fanaticize about a better job or a better home. At the same time, we have the drive and instincts to move toward the next pleasure as fast as we can just like other animals. Also, although we can imagine a lasting perfect state of pleasure, reality always falls short of our expectations. This is probably part of where our idea of heaven comes from. Humans around the world have concretized this perfect, eternal state of blissful tranquility in the ideal of heaven, katastematic pleasure, and its equivalents.

This ideal is known as the *Nirvana principle*. The Nirvana principle, a concept derived from psychoanalytic theory, is the removal of all tension to achieve a stable or organic state. So unlike other animals on this planet, we can imagine things that do not immediately exist in our physical world. This complicates everything.

AREN'T WE MORE THAN JUST PLEASURING SEEKING ANIMALS?

To think that our primary drive is to just go from one pleasurable experience to another is a bit depressing. Surely, we are meant for more than that! Is what psychologists call our *will to pleasure* a grossly reduced and oversimplified conception of what our lives are? Let us look a little deeper into this.

Victor Frankl believed that we are more than that. He was opposed to the idea that our primary drive is pleasure, especially because we can transcend our physical drives and ponder more complex life questions. Frankl also thought that these more advanced contemplative abilities are proof that we were spiritual beings and are divine. This is what sets us apart from other animals. He and many others believed that our ability to imagine a god and a heaven was proof that they existed. This meant that we have a special status among living beings. However, this belief has led many of us to an extremely anthropocentric view of humanity. We justify all kinds of behaviours that have been known to be detrimental to animals and the environment on the basis that humanity is somehow more advanced or higher than other forms of life.

According to Epicurus, the Greek founder of Epicurean philosophy from the fourth century BCE, our contemplative abilities are just another animal adaptation. Like Frankl, he also believed our reasoning abilities were unique among animals. However, Epicurus believed that these abilities did not give us special knowledge of the universe or other levels of existence, it just seems that way to us. Our reasoning abilities are limited powers that just help us to survive in *this* world, like a tiger's claws or a squid's ink. It certainly is not something that places us above the rest of the animal realm. However, it does give us the ability to create systems, have ideas, and think deeply about ourselves.

We humans think about ourselves and our existence in ways that go beyond our immediate biological needs. This ability is what makes us human. With conscious effort, we can step outside ourselves and examine the world. We are *self-reflexive.*

SELF-REFLEXIVITY

Self-reflexivity (sometimes called self-consciousness) is our ability to distinguish and make meaning of phenomena in both our external *and* internal world. We can contemplate ideas such as *past* or *future.* Ideas we cannot see in our immediate physical world. It is to imagine worlds and ideas that do not exist today.

Ernest Becker explains that,

> [Humanity] is a union of opposites, of self-consciousness and of physical body. [Humanity] emerged from the instinctive thoughtless action of the lower animals and came to reflect on [our] condition. [We were] given a consciousness of [our] individuality and [our] part-divinity in creation, the beauty and uniqueness of [our] face and name.[24]

Humans can ask *why*. Why am I feeling this way? Why does the sun come up and go down every day? Why do we exist?

Some theories about how we developed this ability to be self-reflexive are based on brain biology and how we have interacted with nature in the past. For example, the development of our pre-frontal cortex, which led to the combination of our refinement of language and our perception of time, could have given rise to self-reflexivity. However, this ability is not without its problems. Even though we are self-reflexive creatures, we are still bound by our animal nature and our desire for pleasure. The combination of these two characteristics makes us complex creatures indeed!

This is why we believe we are more than just carnal, pleasure-seeking animals. We think that we are "special." Our imaginations seem limitless and our ability to deeply contemplate in this way is unique to us (at least on this planet).

Pierre Teilhard de Chardin, the paleontologist who co-discovered the "Peking Man" fossils, agrees that the main difference between humans and the rest of the animal kingdom is our ability to reflect on our own condition. He describes it as the ability of "consciousness to turn in on itself, to take possession of itself as an object endowed with its own particular consistence and value."[25] Self-reflexivity is a very powerful animal adaptation. Teilhard de Chardin explains that

> The being who is the object of his own reflection, in consequence of that very doubling back upon oneself, becomes in a flash able to raise himself into a new sphere. ...In reality, another world is born. Abstraction, logic, reasoned choice and inventions, mathematics, art, calculation of space and time, anxieties and dreams of love—all these activities of the inner life are nothing else than the effervescence of the newly formed centre as it explodes onto itself.[26]

Thus, our self-reflexivity has exploded into the creation of another world that cannot be seen or touched. It is what Becker calls the *symbolic world*. It is a world created by our minds that did not exist before humans. The symbolic world is made up of myths and stories that we create to give meaning and coherence to our world and lives. It is made up of symbols that represent reality. They help us to make sense of our lives and give us direction for the best ways to live. Myths are the maps of the symbolic worlds we create. They are the stories we tell to make sense of the world going on around us and inside of us.

An example of this is money. Money is just pieces of paper, metal, or sometimes electronic digits on a screen. However, the representations take on very powerful symbolic meaning for us, so much so that we believe that the power lies within the objects themselves rather than the collective idea of money. We are all participating, even if unwillingly, in the story that these nearly worthless bits of metal or paper have actual power in our world.

OUR SYMBOLIC SELVES

We exist in both physical and symbolic worlds. While physically we are blood, bone, tissues, water, and electrical impulses, and not very different from the next human, our symbolic selves are shaped by many factors. Symbolically, we have a name, unique personalities, experiences, and desires. As social constructivists suggest, our identities are co-constructed from the second that we are born through the interaction of our biology and the outside world. Our symbolic selves are what we live out in our culture and society. It is how all the personal, cultural, and societal interactions have come together to create the idea of self and the story of our lives. Our symbolic self is our personal identity.

POWER IN OUR PHYSICAL AND SYMBOLIC WORLDS

In the immediate physical world, we use power to gain pleasure and avoid pain. Just the way all animals do, humans use their strengths and powers to overcome their prey and escape danger. However, humans must also do this symbolically. As self-reflexive creatures, we realize that having power over our symbolic environment is very important for survival and ensuring maximum pleasure. In fact, Nietzsche states that, above all else, living beings use their power to gain favourable conditions for themselves.[27] Jonathan Yahalom takes this idea further by saying that we want power because it is our path to feeling security, and security is needed for us to feel tranquility.[28] Ultimately, we want power so we can gain pleasure and avoid pain.

The most powerful way our self-reflexivity has impacted who we are as humans is that it allowed us to realize that we can manipulate our collective symbolic world to gain personal pleasure and avoid pain. We have discovered that the perceptions we create in our symbolic world can be used to provide us with security in our physical world. This is the basis for many of our individual and collective behaviours as humans.

Consequently, we have come to believe our value is based on how much power we have accumulated in the ways that are recognized by our culture and society. This is why so many of us associate our worth with the size of our bank accounts or the types of products that make others think our wallets are fat. Although the concept of power is symbolic, it feels very real because social and cultural groups collectively agree upon the rules. We gain symbolic power by accumulating symbols. We use representations of power to show the status of individuals.

SELF-ESTEEM: OUR MEASURE OF PERSONAL POWER

Self-esteem is the amount of power we believe we have within a certain context. We start building this symbolic power during our early socialization and continue to do so throughout our lives. Becker believed that self-esteem begins for a child with the first infusion of mother's milk. This warm, supportive, and nourishing experience provides the child with the sense that all is right in the world and radiates a sense of warm satisfaction.[29] If a child's basic physical needs are met without too much effort and distress, they will have a solid foundation for their belief that they have the power to get what they want from their environment—self-esteem. We are not born with our sense of power. It is mostly learned. And how we learned to soothe our childhood insecurities affects how we seek security in the future. As we become adults, we continue to seek symbolic ways of feeding our self-esteem by increasing symbolic power and have found increasingly complex ways of doing so.

Although cars function mainly as a means of transportation in today's world, many of us dream about owning expensive ones that do not necessarily improve on this basic function. This is because expensive cars are symbols of financial success and, therefore, of power. We also desire titles, such as Doctor and CEO, to show that we are a cut above the rest. These titles often symbolize that we possess some knowledge or skill that gives us power in our society. Many of us feel the need to accumulate these symbols almost as much as we need food and procreation. Individually and collectively, we work towards goals that we believe will increase our control over our environments so that we can have more security and pleasure and we do this by accumulating as much symbolic power as possible.

WE NEED MEANING BEYOND PLEASURE AND SECURITY

Leo Tolstoy, a great author and steadfast student of the human condition, wrote in his book *My Confession*, "It is possible to live only as long as life intoxicates us…but as soon as we are sober again, we see that it is all a delusion, a stupid delusion."[30] This is because our self-reflexivity transforms our relatively simple animal desires for pleasure and security into complex ones and our physical world into a symbolic one.

Experiencing constant pleasure is impossible. It never lasts. Instead, we are left with the deep discomfort of feeling that something is missing. That discomfort forces us to keep chasing the perfect state we imagine existing. So, we seek more power. But when all this effort falls short, we begin to question why we cannot achieve the pleasurable states we can imagine. There must be a reason why we cannot experience endless pleasure. We must find something worthwhile and meaningful to do that is not just about immediate carnal pleasure. But how do we find something like this? We need a meaning system, story, or myth that gives us answers to these questions. We need to *re*-story our animal desires to make sense in our complex symbolic world.

MEANING: WHY WE REALLY DO WHAT WE DO

If we really boil it down to its essence, meaning is about maximizing pleasure and minimizing pain in our lives. It is what we have learned is the best path to achieve this. But most of us are not conscious of this essence because meaning is also the symbolic layers of explanation, cultural conditioning, myth, or story that we drape over our basic biological instincts for movement towards pleasure and away from pain. Meaning is about finding something worthwhile to do with our time on this planet, but ultimately, if we think deeply about it, what we find worthwhile always comes down to pleasure and security.

Most of us do not want to believe that maximizing pleasure is the foundation of our personal meanings. We want to believe that there is a more profound explanation to account for our experiences and emotions. But we are not that different from the other animals in this way. The central purpose (or meaning) of their lives is the uncorrupted pursuit of pleasure and the avoidance of pain. The only real difference between us is that they just follow their instincts. However, humans must rationalize and make sense of this pursuit because of our self-reflexive and cognitive abilities. We all have "an individually constructed and culturally based system that makes sense of life and endows it with purpose."[31]

In other words, to make sense of our emotional experience and fit our lives into something larger than ourselves, we create or buy into a story or myth, and the things we do to maximize pleasure, power, and security must be in sync with the stories we are participating in. Whether we are aware of it or not, we all have a meaning system that guides our lives. Joseph Campbell argues that these myths are grand narratives or symbolic worlds that help us to make sense of our existence and how we should live out our daily lives.[32] They are our rulebook or map telling us the most worthwhile ways to live and the choices we should make. But make no mistake, what is worthwhile is ultimately about pursuing pleasure and security, no matter how we choose to dress it up.

Throughout history and today, religions have attempted to provide answers to these big questions and have given us meaning and a context for our desires. For example, in many faiths, endless bliss is found in heaven alone (or its equivalents) and only if we fulfill certain criteria will we get to experience it. Also, the pursuit of pleasure is characterized as evil and something that we should not even want in the first place. But for those of us who cannot accept these answers to life's big questions, we need other explanations, other meanings.

So, what do humans want? No matter how we story it, create myths about it, or rationalize it, all we really want is to be fully engaged, mind, body, and soul, in the chase for optimal pleasure and security. But we also *need* to dress up this chase in symbolic and mythical garb so that it makes sense in our complex, self-reflexive, and symbolic worlds.

DO WE *FIND* MEANING?

Is the meaning we have in our lives something we decided on, or does it already exist and we just have trouble seeing it? Some, like Frankl, feel that we cannot invent meaning but must discover it.[33] This implies that if we just do the right kind of self-exploration, we will find the one "true" meaning of our existence. This also implies that there is an overarching pattern in the universe and each of us, being part of this universal system, has a unique essence or core that can be discovered.[34] In this view, our meaning is already pre-ordained by God, the universe, or even behavioural science, so trying to create a personal meaning is useless.

DO WE *CREATE* MEANING?

While they do not deny the possibility that there is an ultimate cosmic or universal meaning, French philosophers and Nobel Prize winners[1] Albert Camus and Jean-Paul Sartre, argue that we cannot understand it even if it exists. Therefore, we are left with creating our own meaning. Sartre says that if we do not take personal responsibility for creating our own meaning, we are acting in *bad faith*. We are leaving our reason for living in the hands of others; a big no-no to most existential philosophers.[35]

MAYBE IT'S A BIT OF BOTH

We can blend the two as follows. Discovering meaning is the process of reflecting on our lives with the purpose of finding what is profoundly meaningful to *us*. We can connect it to a religious or secular belief about the universe. Maybe it was there all along, hidden or forgotten, or maybe it was not. All we know is that it is personally meaningful to us. We then take that discovered meaning and *create* decisions and actions to live in alignment with it. We align our activities with our purpose, and our purpose is aligned

---

[1]   Sartre was awarded the Nobel Prize but turned it down because of his belief that writers should not be concerned with awards, nor be seen to be as tied to any institutions. Sartre had previously turned down other awards as well.

with who we believe we are. In other words, our meaning is out there for us to discover, but it is our choice whether we use our free will to make it happen.[36]

WE WANT ABSOLUTE ANSWERS

Whether we create meaning, discover it, or both, we can never be certain that we have chosen the right path. We can never really be sure that our meaning system will lead us to more pleasure and less pain. Even with strong religious beliefs, we still debate the will of God or argue with our friends about the meaning of different religious texts. Even when we think we are certain about how to live life, it only takes one impactful experience to completely shift our perspective. This is our problem. No matter how much we want to, we can never be certain that we have chosen the best way to live, the best meaning system, but we still desire an absolute answer.

Uncertainty creates discomfort for us. So, when all our efforts to find a nice, clear purpose ends in more uncertainty, we tend to hang on tight to the best option we have. This could be beliefs inherited from our family, our current religion, or the dominant culture that has seemed to work okay until now. Then, we try to prove that our beliefs *are* the absolute truth by impugning other options. We convince ourselves that beliefs that differ from ours are lesser than, and that those who adhere to them are lesser than.

We rationalize in any way we can that our personal beliefs are superior and somehow more valid than that sub-human group over there.

It makes sense that we desire an absolute meaning system because it eliminates the anxiety and responsibility of having to choose in addition to giving us something of great importance to participate in. In today's complex society, there are almost innumerable choices and decisions to make. But decisions are extremely stressful for people. We are never sure if the choice we have made is the right one. So, when we are presented with something absolute and unquestionable that relieves the stress of having to choose, we hold onto it with all our might.

So we keep searching, moving, and changing because as hard as we try to find something that will provide us with an absolute answer to life, we can never be sure we have found it. Yet we continue the search for a life purpose to relieve us of the "inevitable falling short of our desire for the boundless fullness of existence."[37] However, no meaning system can keep us permanently fulfilled. This is known as *existential paradox*. Reconciling this paradox is really what all of us are trying to do. It is what keeps us motivated in the hope that we will finally find that perfect state of being that we can imagine, and the right meaning system that will get us there. We keep looking for the next experience that will provide us with a moment of contentment. The chase itself, the movement and change, is a foundational part of our existence.

WHY WE FEEL "OFF"

Our powerful imaginations have convinced us that a state of perpetual bliss is possible, just beyond our reach. So, we keep looking for the right formula to get us there. We want a perfect and absolute meaning system that is in sync with our animal desires for maximizing pleasure and security, but our modern world is inhospitable to this desire.

The story of humanity's fall from grace in the Garden of Eden by eating the forbidden fruit from the tree of knowledge could represent the birth of our self-reflexivity. Before that, we lived as the other animals do, never questioning our existence and never feeling a longing for something that is not immediately present. This "fall" was the beginning of our perpetual pursuit to reconcile our imagined perfect bliss with our real experience of life. In an attempt to reconcile this paradox, we have ironically made it more difficult to find meaning and life satisfaction.

This is why it seems that we are so out of sync with the natural world. These days, many of us express an underlying feeling that something is "off" about living in the world. There is a sense that something should be different, but we cannot quite put our finger on it. We are all going through the motions, filling every minute of the day with various activities, but something is keeping us from thriving in the ways we yearn to. We are the proverbial fish out of water and we created this mismatch.

"Wandering re-establishes an original harmony that existed
between human beings and the universe."[38]
— *Bruce Chatwin,* The Songlines

Chapter 2

MEANING FOR PALEO-HUMANS

THE PALEOLITHIC HUMAN

To deepen our understanding of meaning and how we became so mismatched, we must start with what is considered to be humanity's first cultural environment, the Paleolithic era. The Paleolithic era generally refers to the time when humans first appeared (from about 1 million years ago) to about 10,000 years ago with the end of the last ice age and the beginning of agriculture. While in the Paleolithic era our diets were quite diverse depending on the area we lived in, we primarily subsisted by hunting and foraging.

There is a lot of information out there on the benefits of modeling ourselves more closely to our paleo-human ancestors. We compare the differences between our standard, modern diets and the diet of our Paleolithic ancestors. Many who encourage a "Paleo" diet state that our bodies have not evolved much since the Paleolithic era, and therefore, the diet of the paleo-human is the most likely to be the healthiest for us. Although there is a debate around what is the optimal diet for humans, it could be argued that since our biological and psychological mechanisms mainly developed during the Paleolithic era, which represents ninety-nine percent of human history, our psychological baseline is also more aligned with Paleolithic or hunter-gatherer ways of life.[39]

We can explore our paleo-ancestors through biological, anthropological, and sociological lenses, but as we do this, the most important question for our purposes is exploring what made life meaningful and fulfilling for us when we were the paleo-humans. How did we go about the pursuit of maximizing pleasure and minimizing pain? What stories did we tell ourselves about this pursuit and our existence? If we begin with the assumption that the life of the paleo-human serves as the psychophysical baseline for us, then examining what life was like in this era can give us valuable insight into how we experience meaning, purpose, and life satisfaction today.

We exist in a time when the idea of what makes life meaningful gets confused in the haze of the twenty-first-century cacophony. Many voices pull us in various directions and we do not have enough time or energy to sift through the plethora of choices, let alone choose one. This was not the case for us as paleo-humans.

PALEOLITHIC MEANING AND PURPOSE

We cannot go back 20,000 years and ask our hunter-gatherer ancestors about what gave us humans a sense of meaning and purpose in the Paleolithic, but we do have information through anthropological research and the precious interactions with the few remaining foraging tribes left on Earth to help us understand what life was like when we were primarily living as hunters and foragers.

The way our ancestors lived in the Paleolithic environment naturally led to more direct ways of maximizing pleasure and reducing pain. They experienced meaning and purpose directly through their lifestyle. The hunter-gatherer way of being was more in sync with the natural flow of the environment. As a result, we likely experienced far more life satisfaction and happiness in the Paleolithic than we do in the twenty-first century.[40]

In the Paleolithic, we had a more direct experience of life.[41] Our actions were intimately connected to what would increase our chances for survival and increase pleasure. This was not only the satiation of our carnal desires for eating and procreation but also our need for novelty, excitement, community, and movement. Therefore, the Paleolithic environment provided us with a near-absolute and important meaning and purpose—survival.

THE IMMEDIATE RETURN ECONOMY

Whether we want to admit it or not, instant gratification is our genetic heritage. We want pleasure now, not tomorrow. We naturally want to fill the void with anything we can as fast as we can. Thousands of years of evolution have probably programmed us with a gorging gene that creates a biological desire to gorge on food when it is available. While this may be horrific for the diet-conscious modern human to learn, we know that it served us well when food was scarce. It is there for our survival. But this urge goes beyond food and applies to anything that brings us pleasure or reduces pain, both physically and symbolically.

The Paleolithic environment, and lifestyle that came with it, was not only our ideal match for satiating this drive for pleasure, but it also inherently mitigated the pain that sometimes accompanies these urges in the modern world. It was what is called an *immediate return economy,* meaning that the Paleolithic environment provided near immediate gratification for any action that we took.[42] While this term usually applies to procuring food, it can be applied to almost any action we took toward pleasure or reducing pain.

NATURAL WILL POWER

One of the most stressful parts of modern life is resisting our innate desire for instant gratification. At times, we need to perform great feats of willpower and delayed gratification to stay healthy, secure, and successful. We are at a point when we barely need to get off the couch to satiate any desire we can imagine. The modern human is faced with having to resist the urge to eat that pint of ice cream in the fridge; however, as paleo-humans, we would not even have known the concept of "willpower." The lifestyle of hunting and foraging inherently controlled our impulses for instant pleasure and gratification. The environment acted as a built-in moderator for us and delayed potentially destructive urges to a healthy degree for the most part. This is like how smokers on airplanes have little trouble resisting the urge to light up for long flights. It is just not an option. If we had a craving in the paleo-world, we had to work for it by going out and hunting and foraging, so it was almost impossible to overindulge in the long term.

As paleo-humans, we were not met with the constant psychological bombardment of advertisements and messages designed specifically to stimulate our innate impulses. Since we cannot rely on our environment today to help us keep our impulses under control, we have created symbolic barriers to fight our impulses. Some of us today delay gratification through religious justification. For instance, in many religions overindulgence is sinful and delaying gratification or abstaining from such carnal pleasures is pious. Social and cultural acceptance also keeps our desire to indulge our impulses in check. Today, there is a lot of social pressure to reign in our innate desires. However, no matter what symbolic force we use to help us resist our impulses, we must still bear the stress of resisting because there are just so many temptations around us all the time and our symbolic barriers are not always powerful enough compared to the paleo-environment.

At the same time, the environment and lifestyle of our ancestors seemed to provide more immediate gratification of natural pleasures, such as the thrill of the hunt or forage and the camaraderie that came with it. In this way, it was a lifestyle and environment that better matched our physical and psychological needs.

OUR FIRST AND MOST NATURAL OCCUPATION

Canadian author and artist Douglas Coupland felt traumatized by the 9-to-5 and has stated that he is still trying to recover from how barbaric it was.[43] To say that most of us today do not feel passionate about our day jobs is an understatement. Spending so much of our waking lives at jobs we dislike is an affront to life. But this was not always the case. Hunting and foraging were perhaps our first and most natural occupations, our most funda-mental meaning, and the purpose for which our bodies and minds are most suited.[44] In fact, hunting and foraging may be the most perfect human activities because they perfectly blend kinesthetic and katastematic sources of pleasure that the Epicurean philoso-phers talked about.

When we were hunting and gathering, nearly all our desires were immediately returned by the environment; our will to pleasure and will to survive were in sync with each other. And just when a certain territory became overhunted or no longer provided the thrill, we just picked up and moved.

Thus, in addition to the more frequent hunting and foraging for food, the hunter-gatherer lifestyle was ambulatory or nomadic in nature. As paleo-humans, we needed to seek new lands and new hunting grounds to ensure survival. We needed to be curious about what discoveries we might find so we could continue the essential activities of exploring and wandering both physically and psychologically.

Also, as hunter-gatherers we often walked more than 10 km per day with short bouts of intense sprints that were necessary to escape dangerous situations or to pursue prey.[45] Thus, back then we would likely have had a steadier release of endorphins, hormones that both relieve pain and create a general feeling of wellbeing, than many of us do now.[46]

Hunting and foraging were probably the first *peak experiences*. Peak experiences are exciting; deeply moving, exhilarating, and elevated experiences that make us perceive reality differently because our minds, bodies, and emotions are all fully engaged.[47] This is similar to playing in the championship game of a competitive sport, like the seventh game of the Stanley Cup or NBA finals. It is no wonder we still seek peak experiences today. They mimic the hunt.

While the desire to sink our teeth into a fat juicy animal was the goal, the pursuit itself was also exciting and novel. It was never the same. Working together in close-knit groups for the same goal, combined with excitement, novelty, community, movement, and the anticipation of gorging, made us love the process of the hunt as much as the actual catch. We would have died if we did not enjoy it. So not only was the hunt imperative for our survival, but it also ticked all the pleasure boxes.

BEING PRESENT, NATURALLY

Today's world is almost pathologically focused on planning for and anticipating the future. We have one-hundred-year city plans to prepare for changes in the environment. We have fifty-year career and retirement plans. We even plan to colonize Mars sometime in the twenty-second century. We try to map out our entire lives before we live them. Our thoughts and activities fill the future, but our bodies are in the present.

We have always had the ability to plan for and imagine the future, but we were not meant to use this ability very often. Compared to the present, the future is a highly symbolic and imaginary concept. Many of us are more inclined to choose an immediate desire over what might be best for our future selves. This is because the future is not as real to us as the present. As paleo-humans, we spent most of our time with activities that focused on immediate needs for survival in the present or near present. Much of this was because, in the paleo-environment, our needs were more directly met through our physical world than for us in our highly symbolic world today. These tasks were repeated daily and seasonally in a cyclical pattern. As a result, as paleo-humans, we accepted the world "as is" and did not have a symbolic, idealized future we aspired to.[48]

In the Paleolithic, this focus on the present meant there was an acceptance of *what is* because we generally experienced immediate outcomes from our actions. As paleo-humans, we did not have to *try* to live in the present; it was just inherent in our day-to-day existence.

Today, our extreme focus on the future coupled with our symbolic approach to meeting our innate needs have resulted in a collective focus on "growth" or "progress" that did not exist until the agricultural revolution, and certainly was not much of a concern for us as paleo-humans. While there is something to be said for human innovation (and the paleo-human did innovate), our current tendency to be extremely future-focused encroaches on our experience of the present and reduces our ability to live a satisfying life.

THE EXPERIENCE OF TIME AND MEANING

As beings that are programmed by thousands of years of evolution to seek instant gratification, we are genetically predisposed to want our meaning system and our role in it to be temporally in sync with the forces of nature. In other words, we want our internal experience of meaning to match what is happening in the world around us. Consequently, the stories and myths that comprised the paleo-humans' meaning system were more cyclical and rhythmic rather than linear because this is what we observed in nature. In the past, our daily goals were short-term tasks like hunting, which yielded satisfying results in a relatively short time and needed to be repeated regularly. There was also likely a great desire to repeat these tasks since the results came so quickly. That is, our goals were achieved almost every day and our purpose was naturally very process and present-focused.

This very immediate purpose was not focused on some indirect, nebulous long-term goal that seems to make up most people's meaning and purpose today. In general, the longer term a goal is, the more difficult and less satisfying it is for us because we do not receive the reward of feeling consistent and immediate progression and gratification that reinforces the importance of the work and makes us want to continue it.

Nietzsche might have been right when he said that if we have a *why* then we can bear almost any *how*. But it is rare that a long-term goal, which is not directly tied to the survival of ourselves or loved ones, is enough to push us through any unsatisfying activity for very long.

PALEO-CONSCIOUSNESS

Consciousness is the way our minds and bodies experience and interact with the world around us. Paleo-consciousness was forged by thousands of years of living in the wild. The constant location changes, whether because of seasonal migration or the pursuit of new territories, required an openness, alertness, and flexibility of mind that has greatly atrophied in our modern world. Morris Berman suggests that when we began to farm and shifted away from nomadic life in the wild, mental flexibility was lost.[49] Some research suggests that the size of our brains as hunter-gatherers was larger than ours today because our consciousness back then was more in sync with the natural environment.[50] Our brains and psychology were originally meant to acquire and synthesize a wider, deeper, intimate, and more holistic knowledge of our surroundings to survive. It was necessary for hunting, foraging, and living in the wild.

Paleo-consciousness is a universal alertness, vivacity, and imminence that is on multiple aspects of the environment at once.[51] As hunter-gatherers, we had to use our whole field of senses, whereas today, our minds only need to be focused on a few specific aspects of our environment. This paleo-consciousness creates a feeling of heaviness in the present moment.[52] It is acute alertness and connectedness to one's environment. Since an enemy or prey might appear at any time, as hunter-gatherers, our vision and perception had to be everywhere.[53] Ortega Y Gasset describes how a hunter experiences this:

> The air has another, more exquisite feel as it glides over the skin and into the lungs, rocks acquire a more expressible physiognomy and vegetation becomes loaded with meaning... The wind, light, temperature, ground contour, minerals, vegetation all play a part. These elements are not simply there as they are for the tourist, they function and they act.[54]

This ability led to a very different type of knowledge than we have today. In the Palaeolithic era, we had a wide-ranging knowledge about almost everything in our environment, from the behaviours of local animals to the smell of poisonous plants. It was a more holistic knowledge compared to the detached and disembodied learning we experience today.[55] Back then, the natural environment was our classroom and the birds, trees, rocks, and gusts of wind were our teachers. This knowledge gave us all the power we needed to survive in the wild. Unlike much of the knowledge we acquire today, the knowledge we gained as paleo-humans was of direct and immediate use in our day-to-day lives.

This knowledge was far more sense-based than our modern, largely rationally based knowledge. In fact, sense-based perception and knowledge are more in sync with our natural way of being and probably far closer to how and what we are supposed to learn. For example, memory based on sight and smell is more effective for retaining knowledge than through "modern" methods, such as acquiring knowledge through reading.[56] A more "wild" paleo-consciousness led us to experience feelings aligned with the environment and direct participation with all of creation.[57]

Paleo-consciousness rooted us in the here and now, where meaning, movement, and pleasure are one—and the mind is fully engaged. The present moment was all that mattered. This may sound a lot like the tenets of Buddhism, but the difference is that this is natural and inherent, rather than an intentional form of presence. It is being in the flow. It is the environment creating this type of consciousness within us, not the other way around. It is our natural fusing and conforming to our surroundings.

The "heaviness of the present moment" led to our minds and bodies being very engaged in any given moment. Our minds were forced into immediacy as if we were perpetually watching an exciting movie or involved in some competitive sport. Therefore, both Joseph Campbell and Albert Camus agree that the experience of playing competitive sports is a time when we can feel in sync with the world and the most alive. Albert Camus said if he had not fallen ill with tuberculosis at the age of 17, he would have much rather just continued to play soccer with his team in Algiers. This is not to say that sports are the royal road to meaning, purpose, and life satisfaction, but rather, anything that focuses our attention, our mind, and body and makes us hyper-aware of our immediate surroundings, will bring us closer to this paleo-consciousness.

We have all had glimpses of this type of perception and consciousness. Hiking on the mountain at twilight is sure to engage our mind, body, and senses. When being in the wild, it is difficult to think about that stressful meeting next week. How can we when we are listening carefully for wild animals? Just as John Denver sings, "You fill up my senses like a night in a forest." We can speculate that this paleo-consciousness coupled with the more present-focused perception of time may have provided us with a more direct experience of the natural metaphysical movement that underlies all the processes of the universe.

THE SYMBOLIC WORLD OF THE HUNTER-GATHERERS

Many of us remember the children's game "telephone" where one person comes up with a message and then whispers it to the person next to them. Then that person shares the message with the person beside them, and so on. The message goes down the line with so many small changes along the way that by the end it becomes completely different. This is what our symbolic meaning systems are like today. They are an iteration of the original message that has changed so much that our modern symbolic world confuses us to no end. The symbolic world we live in today is based on a symbolic world from some other time, which is also based on some earlier symbolic environment. In the Paleolithic, we were self-reflexive just like we are today, but our symbolic world back then was more directly based on the natural environment and our natural animal instincts.

PALEO-SPIRITUALITY: PARTICIPATING IN THE STORY OF NATURE

Our lives are storied and given meaning through experiences and interactions with our environment. Today, much of this environment is a confused and complicated symbolic world we have created in our minds. As a result, the stories we create about our world and ourselves are over-complicated. While some of us may carry similar belief systems that include deep participation with nature and the universe as a whole, because of the mismatch between our day-to-day existence and our original paleo-lifestyle, we do not feel it down to our bones like we did back in the Paleolithic era.

In the Paleolithic past, our personal stories and view of the world were largely based on what we witnessed and experienced in the flow of nature. It was a paleo-spirituality. Spirituality is the way we narrate and explain our pursuit of pleasure and our existence in the universe. Paleo-spirituality was based on external observations instead of internal rationalizations. What was considered "good" was not derived from a future-oriented system of ethics but from the ways animals, plants, rocks, mountains, and even the wind affected us. We categorized them as good or bad depending on how we associated them with experiences of pleasure or pain. Our daily experiences were guided by our instincts for survival and our stories and meanings were born out of our experiences.

Back then, we viewed nature as something we could trust to guide our lives. Why not? Nature must have seemed miraculous and effortless. Nature provided everything that all beings needed, and all beings seemed to work in harmony. It was also *alive*. Everything in nature is animated, moving, and in flux. Rocks, plants, and animals participate in this world just as much as we do. In fact, the traditional Sioux believe that animals and nature reveal much of the mysterious Creator's ways.[58] We could trust the ways of these other beings because they were equal and integral parts of the whole story of nature.

In the paleo-world, our cravings for the immediate return of our desires were satisfied not only by our relationship with nature but also by our symbolic meaning system. Because our symbolic meaning system was based on our direct participation with the natural world and our natural instincts, it easily rang true and was reinforced in nearly every moment. This means our instincts for pleasure and security were in sync with our personal and cosmic meaning. The resulting congruence between the physical, rational, and spiritual realms would have diminished any longing for some better place or time.

Conversely, many modern humans, especially those who are atheistic or agnostic, lack the satisfaction of feeling in sync and therefore suffer from a yearning for something better. This may be why today we spend a significant amount of time thinking about some blissful afterlife or future. As paleo-humans, we would not have focused our efforts on striving for another reality or on "high" gods as much as us future humans do.[59]

Also, in the paleo-world, we did not focus so much attention on pleasing high gods or seeking higher spiritual planes because there were fewer large systems of invisible rules that governed our lives. Instead, we lived by the rules of nature that we observed. In fact, Berman suggests that for many hunter-gather cultures there was a general acceptance of death and no hope of an afterlife, at least in the Christian sense of a "better" place.[60]

Back then, our spirituality was not about reaching some sort of enlightened state or about allaying the fear of death but was centred on being part of the flow of life and the universe rather than trying to escape it. Although the fear of death existed, it was likely accepted as a part of the life cycle that could be observed everywhere. Compared to today, we took our cues from nature and accepted the world as is without trying to change it or escape from it. This type of spirituality would have provided a more instant spiritual gratification in the sense that there was no need to strive to reach another place, time, or altered state to gain its benefits. We did not experience great stress in trying to figure out what to do with our time. Just like other aspects of the hunter-gatherer life experience that were more direct, so too was paleo-spirituality. It was a real experience of the world rather than the layers of rationalizations and abstractions that make up our worldviews today.

CHOICES AND FREEDOM

A major source of anxiety in our postmodern, relativistic world is the freedom and immense availability of choice. While the sheer number of choices necessary for life today can be crippling for many, the experience of life in the paleo-environment was so present-focused that most of the stress related to freedom of choice would not have been present. Undoubtedly, there were decisions to be made in our paleo-world, but they would not even come close to the number of decisions we are faced with today.

When we lived in the paleo-environment, we did not have to choose between thousands of occupations to figure out which one was most suited to us. For example, if we decided to hunt to the north one day instead of the east and no game was found, the choice could easily be remedied. But today, if we choose to be a lawyer, we could spend seven years in school only to realize that we despise it and want to become an accountant instead. Another four years! We did not have to choose a system of meaning or spirituality among hundreds of possibilities. Instead, our lives were focused on essential tasks that were carried out in the present within a meaning system formed in relationship with our environment and instincts.

Jean-Paul Sartre famously said that humans are "condemned" to be free. We want choice, but ironically, too much choice wreaks havoc on our psychology as we try to figure out which choice will give us the most pleasure in the future. To complicate this, we have existential guilt when we regret the choices we did not make. Many of us carry so much anxiety trying to figure out our meaning and purpose in life that it has become almost pathological. We get paralyzed with indecision and never move very far in one direction. Just like Maddie from the beginning of this book, so many of us suffer from this burden of choice and responsibility. So, it is not that we cannot make choices, (our ancestors made choices every day), but back then our choices did not carry the weight of symbolic responsibility, time investment, or money like they do today.

POWER AND SELF ESTEEM

Imagine that the knowledge we possessed and actions that we took almost always yielded the results we wanted. We would feel so powerful! Believe it or not, this innate sense of confidence is much closer to our genetic heritage and our natural way of being than we think. However, today, when we have a difficult choice to make, we often look to outside sources for knowledge and advice, for something or someone to guide us. We seek a power that is outside of ourselves to tell us the right decision so that we can feel secure.

Many cultural and societal factors in our world today have led to the belief we need to spend much of our lives seeking symbolic power such as fame, positions of authority, and great riches. If these things are threatened, we must do what we can to protect them including harming others along the way. We have been conditioned to think this is necessary and normal, but it is not. As paleo-humans, we did not need to go to extreme means to gain power and security in the environment. Like our other impulses, the will to power was kept at levels more natural to us.

As I mentioned in the first part of this book, our sense of power and self-esteem are closely tied to our real and perceived ability to have control over our environment to satiate our desires. When we believe that we will be able to satisfy our psychological and physical needs through our actions, we do not feel the need to seek any more power. As paleo-humans, our sense of power over our environment and life was frequently reinforced in our day-to-day life, so we did not need to seek much more. We hunted or foraged and often got what we needed. We had a lot of trust in our environment and our abilities. [61]

When we were hunter-gatherers, there was no worry that we needed to progress or accumulate more because we had a trust that the world would provide meaning, gratification, and satisfaction for us. There was not as much need as today to think about personal progress and power because our lives were already in sync with our meaning system. We had relatively simple needs that were met in a more immediate sense.[62] As we will learn later, the idea of "progress," in a culturally significant and symbolic way, only really comes along in the agricultural revolution.

PALEOLITHIC CHILDREARING

The immediate return on our efforts undoubtedly helped us develop innate feelings of power. However, another important way we acquired a sense of personal power was through hunter-gatherer childrearing practices. As paleo-children, we learned that the world around us provided what we needed without too much psychological effort. The parenting practices that were common in the Paleolithic likely led to more secure parent-child attachment, which provided us, as paleo-children, with the belief that our needs would be met relatively easily.[2] As paleo-children grew up, we carried this sense of power and security with us into older childhood and adulthood. In addition, while modern humans

---

2   Berman argues that hunter-gatherer child-rearing practices of birth spacing, late weaning, caregiver proximity, and somatic holding enabled paleo-children to have a more secure attachment to their caregivers and environment.

have transitional objects such as blankets and stuffies, the environment itself, such as the trees, were transitional objects for children in the paleo-environment because we knew the environment would provide for our needs.[63]

POWER IN PALEO-SOCIETY

Most hunter-gather societies were fiercely egalitarian and "horizontal," as opposed to the vertical and hierarchical structures that prevail in our society today. Even though some members of these groups no doubt held more social esteem because they were skilled hunters or foragers, anthropologists insist that most tribes used *leveling mechanisms* to ensure that no one member gained too much power in the group.[64] For example, when a hunter or group of hunters came back with a great kill, it was customary to poke fun at the size of the catch, degrading the achievement. Most of the time, the hunters did not feed themselves until all the other members got their share. Thus, even if we thought we had contributed more to the group, we would be "structurally" reminded of the value and equality of all members.[65] We seemed to know that if one person gets it in their head that they are more important or valuable, it could be destructive to the whole group. So jealously, disappointment, and longing related to comparison were lessened.

Also, when different types of roles within a group are valued, then people tend to feel more free to choose a role within the group that actually suits them as opposed to seeking something that might give them more value, self-esteem, and power. In other words, since extreme levels of power were mitigated, every role in a hunter-gatherer society was of near equal esteem, necessary for the group's survival, and valued for its contribution to the group. In this way, as paleo-humans, our skills and personality were much more matched to whatever our role was in society than most of us today.

In the paleo-world, not only did we have a lot of trust in our environment from a young age, but we also learned through daily reinforcement that we had a lot of innate power to get what we needed. So, it was a double whammy of psychological security—high self-esteem and high trust in the environment. In modern times, however, we see less secure individuals continue to seek more power or to create different meanings beyond survival in order to create psychological security. It follows that, in the Paleolithic, with less uncertainty about ourselves and our world, there was little need to seek absolute answers about life or to depend on a higher source for validation and psychological security.

CONCLUSION

So, can we somehow go back to this baseline of meaning when our natural desires to maximize pleasure were more in sync with the world we lived in? No, probably not. Maybe with great psychological effort we could move closer to it as individuals, but the crushing weight of modern society, culture, and ten thousand years of "progress" that led to our modern world would make it exceedingly difficult, if not impossible. However, this foray into the past was not purely nostalgic. It has provided us a base to understand how and when our psychophysical mismatch began. As we shall see, the seed of this mismatch can be found in the agricultural revolution.

"By going sedentary, we shifted from a direct experience of life to the pursuit of substitutes."[66]
— *Morris Berman,* Wandering God

Chapter 3

MEANING IN THE AGRICULTURAL REVOLUTION

The Paleolithic was the era when humans experienced the most sustainable and satisfying meaning because our lifestyles, DNA, spirituality, and environment were matched. This shifted with the Neolithic era, or what is known as the agricultural revolution. The irony of this "revolution" is that although it allowed us to produce more food, it was a false victory in terms of human happiness and sustainable meaning. With the advent of agricultural production, feeding a growing population became less of a problem, but our meaning, purpose, and very existence became a growing one.

The Neolithic age roughly refers to the period beginning about 10,000 years ago when sedentary settlements and agriculture become more prevalent. This is also the period when urban areas and more complex civilizations begin to develop, bringing with them more complex lives.

FROM FORAGING TO FARMING

Why exactly we decided to drop our spears and arrows and pick up hoes and begin to farm is a topic of much debate. Some scholars attribute the agricultural revolution to shifting climatic patterns that led to changes in the Earth's flora and fauna. Others attribute it to a slow and steady population increase that could no longer be sustained on hunting and gathering alone. In the end, it was probably a constellation of factors that led to the fateful shift. However, why this happened is not what we are interested in, but what effect this had on meaning and how it made us mismatched and out of sync with ourselves and the environment.

How we go about feeding ourselves shapes our lives more than any other factor and so the agricultural revolution is arguably the most monumental event in human history. It set us on a path of what is called *evolutionary mismatch*, when our lifestyles were no longer in sync with our DNA.[67] Most of us have learned the view that agriculture is an exemplar of human progress because it led to great civilizations. However, as we shall see, while it may have helped us to grow in population, it drastically reduced our quality of life and increased our experience of existential crisis and paradox.

INDIRECT EXPERIENCE OF LIFE & DELAYED GRATIFICATION

After the major shift in how we fed ourselves, several changes followed that immensely impacted how we experienced our entire lives. In the Paleolithic, our meaning was all about the direct gratification of our survival instincts in the immediate present. However, as Neolithic farmers, we went from experiencing life directly to pursuing substitutes, and consequently, the need to delay gratification.[68]

The first of these changes is that farming is not nearly as gratifying as the hunt or forage. That rush of excitement and subtle fear when we spotted a fat wild boar was gone. The novelty of spending our time in the direct pursuit of food and security, the foundational experience of being alive, was gone. These experiences gradually dissipated and were replaced with knock-offs. We went from being participants to spectators, active to passive. The meal was now separate from the hunt. Life became dull and the visceral connection to daily tasks diminished.

FUTURIZATION: PLEASURE DELAYED

Planting a seed does not immediately satisfy or thrill us, nor does it make us feel powerful and secure like the piercing of an animal's flesh. With the focus on agriculture, these natural desires for pleasure and security are pushed to the future or even eliminated. Our psychophysical need to maximize pleasure and minimize pain that was once satisfied in the present as paleo-humans is increasingly delayed and deferred to some future time for us as Neolithic farmers.

In the Neolithic, our actions no longer yielded survival and satisfaction directly, like the hunt or the forage. Sure, we planted the seed, but then it was a waiting game and a worrying game. Not only were the natural excitement, directness, and immediacy of living as a hunter-gather gone, but to ensure survival, we also had to complete tasks that would ensure our survival that would not bear fruit for another year or more. Our anxiety grew as our hopes were pinned on the success of the harvest far in the future.

Also, the direct pleasure of spending our days with like-minded others in pursuit of daily sustenance gave way to more individual and single household activities. While there was most certainly a sense of community with other farmers and extended family, the daily camaraderie of a group of foragers seeking the basics of survival was gone.[69] Yet the desire to experience the pleasure of being part of a meaningful community continued for us.

Boredom and ennui also became more of a feature of the Neolithic because we went from a nomadic way of life to a sedentary one. Not only were the daily forays into the wild gone but seasonal migrations gave way to fixed locations. We became stuck in one place and our natural desire for novelty and change was stunted.

FUTURIZATION: THE LOSS OF POWER AND TRUST

Planting seeds did not make us feel as powerful and secure as we did when we hunted. In the Neolithic, we worried. We had to find ways to reassure ourselves that the seeds would be okay, that we would survive. Trust in the environment and oneself gave way to distrust, fear, and dependency. While as hunter-gatherers, we were certainly dependent on the environment and weather events, as farmers, we were far more so.[70] If the farmer had a bad yield, we could not pick up and go to a new farm on a whim. We would have to wait an entire year to try it all over again. We had to plan at least a year in advance and budget out our crop from the last harvest. All our eggs were in one basket, and it was a basket we did not have a lot of control over. This led to a delayed or deferred sense of security and power. At the same time, our cultivated and tamed fields were cordoned off from nature, and the wild beyond the fence that we were once intimately connected with, became something to fear.

During this time, our sense of power over and trust in the environment decreased and our psychological need for security increased. We felt the need for power but because we could not find it within ourselves any longer, we needed to find it somewhere else. We needed to find something that would help us get power over the environment to allay our anxiety and fear.

In some ways, as the Neolithic farmers, we probably felt that we had freed ourselves of the whims of the hunt and forage and when the harvest was good, celebrated this newfound "human" way of feeding ourselves. It may have seemed that we had gained a sense of stability and security, but in doing so we also separated and isolated ourselves from the wild environment's natural care. Like a teenager who wants their independence but does not yet know the heavy weight of that responsibility, we left the comfort and protection of the natural world to strike out on our own in a new and frightening world.

Now we had to secure the future for ourselves. And while we could think (and plan and worry) far into the future, we were not all that psychologically equipped to deal with the consequences of that, so we sought to minimize our fears and anxiety over the future by creating a new meaning system based on our new isolated and frightening status quo.

THE NEED FOR MORE COMPLEX MEANING SYSTEMS

"Life goes on, long after the thrill of living is gone" are the iconic lyrics by John Mellencamp in the song *Jack and Diane*. This sentiment may reflect how we felt as Neolithic farmers when we no longer lived as in sync with nature as in the Paleolithic. In the Neolithic era, our pursuit of survival became separated from our natural will to power and pleasure.

As hunter-gatherers, our meaning system and symbolic world were directly based on what we observed in nature and within ourselves. As a result of this, we reified those natural instincts. In other words, our meaning system was informed by our daily experiences in the wilds of nature. However, because living in an agricultural world required us to delay gratification of the will to pleasure, we were now profoundly out of sync with nature and our natural inclinations. So rather than our meaning system being based on natural ways of being, our Neolithic meaning system was now based on how to maximize pleasure and reduce pain in this new human-made environment that is characterized by the need to delay gratification, and where power was increasingly outside ourselves. We also needed to make sense of why our lives were not as satisfying as we could imagine. As farmers, we could neither follow our natural instincts nor satiate our desires to maximize pleasure and minimize pain in the immediate present as we could in the Paleolithic. Yet, we still had that same desire for instant gratification, so we needed to somehow make sense of this new and uncomfortable predicament.

The experience of securing our survival became a lot more psychologically complex in the Neolithic. As Neolithic humans, our anxiety increased because our survival hinged on the precarious outcome of the harvest. We needed to regain our sense of power and security in our new way of being and in ourselves. We needed a way to minimize the pain and insecurity. We needed to mitigate the loss of faith in the providence of the environment to provide sustenance. We tried to do this by accumulating power and security in an increasingly symbolic world.

VERTICALIZATION: THE TRANSFER OF POWER THROUGH MYTH AND STORY

It would have been obvious to us as Neolithic farmers that nature had tremendous power over our survival and there was not a lot we could do physically to ensure we could feed ourselves. This is why Berman suggests that agriculture led to the *verticalization* of spirituality in which we began perceiving ourselves as "lower" than and separate from many of the forces of nature we feared, and at the same time, felt much more dependent on them than in the

Paleolithic. It became increasingly necessary to use our powers of abstraction and storytelling to make sense of our new relationship with the world around us. We created new myths, but unlike our myths in the Paleolithic that were based on our harmonious coexistence with nature, our new myths needed to help explain why we felt out of sync and what we could do about it. For example, the wind, which may have been a fickle nuisance in the Paleolithic, became a god that needed to be feared and appeased in the Neolithic.

On top of that, after the agricultural revolution, we had to theorize the best way to gain the favour of the gods and then had to live by those human-made and symbolic rules. We began to pay more attention to and analyze the behaviour of the different forces of nature or gods as they related to conditions for an abundant harvest. While much of our life as farmers was filled with chores around the farm, it was also infused with the extra layer of anxiety thinking about how our actions would affect crops and lives. "Am I doing right by God?" "Will the crops fail if my daughter goes unwed?" These types of questions would have been far more prevalent for us in the Neolithic. We had become symbolically and psychologically dependent, and our actions, at least in part, were no longer driven by natural inclinations but by the imagined will of a god and fear of the environment.

When spirits became gods, the shamans became priests. In the Paleolithic, we had access to knowledge of the natural world's forces, but in the Neolithic, this knowledge and its rules became concentrated in a few select individuals. This is because new cosmic meaning systems are built on layers of abstraction and logic as opposed to real-world experience. So, in the same way that we transferred the will to power onto gods, we also began to transfer power onto those who best understood these gods.

THE COSMIC HUNT

Besides figuring out how to tap into the power of these new gods, we also used stories to explain why our desire to have pleasurable, exciting, and novel experiences went largely unfulfilled. We felt the need to gorge but at the same time, had to resist so we would not use up all our harvest. Thus, we needed to come up with increasingly compelling reasons for why we should resist our urges.

The focus on higher planes of existence and more powerful beings, combined with our desire for immediate pleasure and excitement, led to seeking altered states and trances in the name of connecting with those higher planes. This became our new goal. It was our new hunt. A cosmic hunt. It was the ultimate of trying to fuse ourselves with a powerful other for pleasure and security because, without our direct interconnection with nature in time and space, we no longer felt powerful ourselves. The psychological need for security and fusion increased to the point that seeking communion with gods became even more important than feeding ourselves. This is when fasting and delaying the gratification of our desires as spiritual practices would have become more commonplace. Hence, the symbolic world overtakes the physical.

Our new cosmic meaning system, based on higher planes and beings rather than nature, came with a new system of ethics based on the imaginary symbolic world we had created. Ethics were no longer based on our direct interaction with the natural world. Meaning was no longer directly related to pursuing naturally pleasurable activities. Instead, basic survival became increasingly separate from pleasure and power. Farming would not directly provide us with these, so we created a symbolic world that would. Eventually, we created a place that gave us a purpose for delaying gratification with the promise of the most power, security, and pleasure our minds could fathom.

HEAVEN: OUR NEW "WHY"

Rather than survival and immediate gratification, we now had a new goal, one that we had to convince ourselves was worth working and suffering toward. A new myth that would guide us even if it was not as satisfying. It led us to a place where all this delayed gratification was worth it because we made it an essential determinant for making it to heaven. The urges that we shared with wild animals became taboo and shameful. The wolf eats whatever it wants, when it wants, why is it that we cannot? The wolf must be lesser than. For many, natural urges would have become evil and asceticism a virtue. Our primary goal in the Neolithic was our pursuit of pleasure and power in heaven and symbolically protecting and separating ourselves from wild nature. Thus, heaven became the ultimate of delayed gratification, verticalization, and futurization. At the same time, with hours filled with farming, our daily lives became mundane.

So, we had a meaningful purpose in the Neolithic, but it was not as naturally satisfying or sustainable as that of the Paleolithic. The feeling of existential paradox, that "inevitable falling short of our desire for the boundless fullness of existence" increased even more because that perfect blissful state was pushed far into the future and up into the clouds.[71] But rather than go "backwards" to the Paleolithic ways of life for the best means to reconcile the widening gulf and increasing dissatisfaction, most of us in Neolithic societies doubled down on our new abstract and derivative meaning systems leading to what is called the *Axial Age.*

THE AXIAL AGE: THE HEIGHT OF THE AGRICULTURAL REVOLUTION

As agricultural societies grew larger and more complex, our meaning systems changed to keep up. We needed our worldview to match the world around us. The simpler ideas of the early Neolithic and Paleolithic no longer sufficed to explain life in these more complex civilizations. Now enters the Axial age.

The Axial Age was a time of seeking new ways of understanding ourselves, our place in the universe, and our increasing feelings of existential paradox. It was the time when Siddhartha Gautama sat underneath the Bodhi tree and achieved enlightenment. It was when Lao Tzu, the keeper of archives, hurriedly scribbled out what would become the *Tao Te Ching* in exchange for permission from the warden of the Han Ku Pass to leave the dynasty. And it was when Socrates, Plato, and Aristotle walked the streets of Athens, building the foundation of Western philosophy.

The quest for new meanings and new explanations was further facilitated by an increasing leisure class, who had a lot more time to think, but who experienced even more existential paradox despite more and more privilege and options for living. Hence, all the great schools of philosophy focused on finding the best way to live. Karl Jaspers, who coined the term Axial Age, describes it:

> What is new about this age is that [humans] become conscious of Being as a whole, of [ourselves] and [our] limitations. [We] experience the terror of the world and [our] own powerlessness. [We] ask radical questions. Face to face with the void

[we] strive for liberation and redemption. By consciously recognizing [our] limits [we] set [ourselves] the highest goals. Big questions that were specifically psychological in nature emerged: "Who am I?" and "Why are people different?"[72]

Why is there a gulf between what I can imagine and what I experience? These questions are the maturation of existential paradox that had always existed but had become far more pressing. Therefore, the Axial Age is when there was a certain level of psychological, spiritual, or philosophical development precipitated by the increasing complexity of society and the experience of existential paradox. But what was on one level a triumph of human abstraction and rational thinking, on another level was also a trap for our minds.

THE BURDEN OF LIFE BEYOND SURVIVAL

With the new development of cities, those of us experiencing life away from farming may have believed that we had further freed ourselves from the caprices of nature, but just like our shift from hunting and gathering to agriculture, this too was a false victory that exacerbated and complicated existential paradox even more.

This newfound freedom from farming meant a growing portion of society did not have to worry nearly as much about how they were going to survive and feed themselves. This seems like progress, but once biological survival was secure, our lives became even more of a puzzle. In fact, we may not be equipped to deal with the psychological burden of figuring out how to live life beyond survival. The resulting psychological discomfort drives us to find something as worthwhile as survival to focus on, but that may not exist. At the same time, we must convince ourselves that the way we spend our lives is of great importance, or else with so much time on our hands and finding nothing worthwhile to do, we lapse into boredom, what Leo Tolstoy describes as the desire for desires.

INEQUALITY, COMPARISON, AND PERSONAL MEANING

While it certainly would not seem like it to us in the twenty-first century, when we lived in the Axial Age, we had a lot more choices than we did in the Paleolithic or early Neolithic. Also, the increasing population led to even more verticalization of society, which resulted in more hierarchy and the development of a class system. The relative equality of the Paleolithic gave way to more inequality.[73] This was another source of life dissatisfaction. As a result of this inequality, the comparison of our lives to others had a significant effect on meaning and purpose. Even if most us in the Axial Age believed in some sort of reified hierarchy, seeing others in our community who were more affluent was bound to lead to more comparison and dissatisfaction. So, meaning and purpose became more about what we *wanted* in our lives rather than what we *needed*. Consequently, we needed to buy into a meaning system that explained the reasons for that gulf between the life we saw others enjoying and our own. For example, both the Brahmin, the highest-ranked of the classes in traditional Hindu society and monarchs of Medieval Europe were given their status by God. But whether we believed this new inequality was justified by a new meaning system or not, our expectations for life in the Axial Age would have gone through the roof.

Even with this new purpose of striving for what others had and finding justification for the inequality we saw, we still innately desired pleasure and security. If we believed others had more pleasure and security than we did, we would set our sights on having what they do whether in this life or the next. In other words, no matter how we dressed it up with new myths and stories, we still desired objects and symbols that we believed would result in more pleasure and security. However, because those pleasures and security were either off in a different spiritual realm or high up on the hierarchy of society, our personal life satisfaction would have greatly decreased.

Trying to increase our status in a hierarchy would have become a worthy goal since we thought it would lead to more pleasure and security. It may be that the Axial Age gave birth to the original "keeping up with the Joneses" concept since there were more levels of people to compare ourselves to than ever before. If we know there is more that we can have, we want it. As the societal gap grew, the spiritual meaning system changed to reflect and explain it. That is, the positions in society were increasingly reified and justified through often abstract and spiritual means, both to help those in powerful positions stay in them and to justify the symbolic hierarchy for others. The meaning system reflected what we experienced in the world and reinforced it for us.

KNOWLEDGE AND CHOICES: A DOUBLE-EDGED SWORD FOR MEANING

With the growth of population after agriculture and increasing urbanism, which gave rise to cities like Babylon, Athens, Alexandria, and Xian, human occupations became more specialized than ever before in human history. From the Neolithic and then Axial Age, we became specialized experts in certain tasks. Up to that point, there were very few choices for what we did with our lives. But the complexities of societies during the Axial Age necessitated a diversification of roles. No longer did we have to hunt, gather, or farm for survival. Now we could be a shoemaker, a banker, a cleric, a market stall owner and many other occupations that popped up as needed. This was probably one of the first times in human history when at least some of us had to choose the way we lived. Jobs became more detached from bare survival and our meaning and purpose for living became even more abstract.

The Axial Age also gave rise to the first writing systems. First, the cuneiform system developed in Sumer around 3200 BCE, then Egyptian hieroglyphs. This development was not necessarily the result of a stroke of genius, but because writing became necessary as information became more complex and needed to be recorded. Writing did not have much use for hunter-gatherers or early farmers, but as societies grew and communities expanded, we needed to, for example, find a way to record the amount of grain stored and to whom it belonged. The amount of information needed for society to run smoothly required a "memory" more powerful than any human possessed. Thus, writing took human societies to the next level of symbolization and abstraction. It gave birth to complex philosophies and gospels. Now our symbolic world could be put in physical form: books.

The maximization of pleasure, power, and security became even more verticalized, abstract, and indirect than in the early Neolithic era. We began to have access to vast amounts of knowledge and sought more than just a stable existence. We now searched for a "higher" truth in philosophy and complex religion. Since just having more food and luxury did not satisfy us anymore, we became motivated to find something that would—transcendence. We created castles in the sky and invented a system of behaviour to reach them. Our meaning systems became more arcane with complex doctrines. Meaning and purpose became about fighting for something worthwhile beyond bare existence as living and survival became easier and life became more comfortable. All of this gave rise to a very different experience of consciousness.

AXIAL CONSCIOUSNESS: TOWARDS AN INNER WORLD

Consciousness is our perception and awareness of life. It is how we look at the world and ourselves. At the same time, it is a product of our culture and environment. One of the major changes that happened during the Axial Age is that because we started living in urban environments, we relied far less on nature as the basis for understanding the world. The natural lifecycle no longer provided the template of life. Out of sight, out of mind. Life was now lived more internally in abstract meaning systems and how we saw the world was increasingly influenced by people and ideas, rather than by nature.

Our consciousness became even more self-reflexive, analytical, and future-focused than in previous eras. Put in another way, our consciousness became indirect. Our minds were no longer directly in the flow of nature as they once were. During the Paleolithic, we were primarily concerned with the gratification of physical desires for survival, but in the Axial Age, we developed a compulsion to pursue symbolic satisfaction. Our perception was filtered through abstract religion, writing, and symbolism.

THE PROBLEM OF EXISTENCE

For the first time in human history, there was a group of us in each society whose very purpose was to examine human existence with our intellect rather than through day-to-day observations in nature. A very abstract meaning and purpose, indeed! Within this category are the great schools of ancient philosophy, such as the Stoics and the Epicureans, who would spend their days contemplating the nature of existence. This was the beginning of the transition from mythical cultures and meaning systems to more rational ones—the first complex philosophical and religious systems. In Greece, this was the transition from the Olympic gods to the systemic philosophy of Aristotle. It was also the transition from largely orally based spiritualities to ones based on scriptures. In the Axial Age, there were whole, often competing groups who dedicated their lives to discovering the best way to live, why life had become a problem, and how to achieve that age-old goal of optimizing pleasure and security. We needed to scratch an itch that we created ourselves, and just like poison ivy, the more we scratched, the itchier it got.

All the abstractions and philosophical systems seemed at first to be the best path to solving the problem of our existence. We thought we finally understood our world and how to achieve happiness. We had separated ourselves from nature and we now just had to follow the prescriptions of whatever abstract meaning system we created. Alas, these great philosophical or spiritual systems only created more contradictions.

We began to feel the heaviness and strangeness of our existence far more than our Paleolithic ancestors ever did. Leaving the wild comfort and camaraderie of nature, our existential isolation increased, and we fervently examined this condition that we inadvertently created. We got trapped in our own abstract and arcane worlds. That small splinter in our mind became a chasm, a void—an existential void. Our goal was to reconcile this paradox and to bring ourselves back in sync, but that attempt proved futile.

"The postmodern human exists in a universe whose significance is at once utterly open and without warrantable foundation."[74]
— *Richard Tarnas,* The Passion of the Western Mind

Chapter 4

MEANING IN THE TWENTIETH & TWENTY-FIRST CENTURIES

God was pronounced dead by Friedrich Nietzsche in the early 1880s after a long and courageous battle with existential paradox.[75] It was not just the Christian God that was lost, but all those arcane spiritualties and philosophical systems that were born in the Axial Age. The same ones that worked for years as a way to mask existential paradox and to make sense of the world no longer sufficed as meaning systems for the modern world. Their principles could no longer explain the new world that was emerging. Again, our meaning systems needed to change.

The human soul's search for fullness, excitement, and satiation of the will to pleasure was once satisfied through the wild thrill of the hunt and a meaning system that was aligned with our innate desires. Then, after the agricultural revolution, this thrill was deferred to the domain of high gods and a distant heaven. We did not trouble ourselves with trying to achieve a blissful life since we knew that as long as we followed the rules and made it through the suffering on Earth, heaven was waiting for us when we died.

THE EROSION OF ABSOLUTE FAITH

New ideas began to trickle into Europe, first via Silk Road traders, and then around 1100 CE through the Crusades that were meant to, ironically, solidify the Christian faith. Through Middle Eastern scholars, Europeans rediscovered the philosophy of ancient Greece and Rome that had been largely lost to the Dark Ages. This led to the erosion of absolute faith in the Christian church and we began to seek alternative ways of seeing humanity and the world. In turn, this led to Renaissance Humanism, the Enlightenment, and the Scientific and Industrial Revolutions that further eroded the West's absolute faith in high gods and heavens while also providing us with a more abundant life. We, the humans of the nineteenth, twentieth, and twenty-first centuries, arrived at a new existential and postmodern threshold.

We began to seek pleasure directly again as we once did in the Paleolithic, but this time, we did not live in the natural environment or have a high god to rely on to provide context and guidelines for this pursuit. Without God or a spear, the West entered a new and frenzied search to fill the void that the death of God had left. We were finally free of nature *and* God! The will to pleasure was stripped of any mythical garb and laid naked before us. It is not just in the West that these grand narratives began to crumble. In China, thousands of years of largely Confucian-influenced dynastic rule came to an end on February 12, 1912, after over a century of decline.

FEELING ALONE: THE RISE OF EXISTENTIALISM

The age of existentialism was when we became conscious of the human predicament without the security of God or nature. Alone in the universe, with no grand story or narrative to hold on to, the responsibility to secure our lives is placed squarely back on our shoulders. Rather than puzzling out the metaphysical problems, we turned inward. In fact, many of the figures we associate with existentialism would not have even considered themselves philosophers, but were writers, artists, theologians, and therapists—masters of the human experience.

While for thousands of years, small undercurrents of nihilism (the idea that the universe and life have no ultimate meaning) had existed, they never took hold in any way that affected the overall zeitgeist of their time. It was in the nineteenth century we began to deeply feel what William James called the "worm at the core" of the human condition.[76] This worm at the core is our desire to experience the fullness of life, tranquility, an absolute meaning, and eternal life that was once promised by God and heaven that we now found dubious—the inevitable falling short of the existential perfection we could imagine and for which we are now solely responsible.

The feeling of being alone in the universe and making sense of our existence became forefront in our minds. While some continued to turn to high gods or other metaphysical absolutes to provide a "heaven on Earth," most of us slowly began to feel that we, as individuals, were largely responsible for ensuring the kind of life that we wanted. We felt that we alone were responsible for maximizing pleasure in our own lives since there was no absolute and larger meaning to guide us.

Alone in the universe with no one to reconcile existential paradox but ourselves, Nietzsche's new concept called the *Ubermensch* (superman or super-human), was created. This was essentially a symbolic representation of the will to power being transferred back to humans. The power and security that God provided for us were gone, so to fill this vacuum, we created a new myth and meaning system. One that told us that maximizing pleasure and minimizing pain was our responsibility and that we had to exert our own power to achieve it.

Meaning in the nineteenth, twentieth, and twenty-first centuries is often thought of in terms of a *crisis* of meaning because it is difficult to have a sustainable cosmic meaning system based on human power alone. However, it is not so much a crisis as it is an *excess* of meaning that is the true predicament. What we are doing now to deal with our feelings of being mismatched with the world is creating innumerable "offerings" that are available for us everywhere and whenever we need them. Essentially, we are trying to create a world of instant gratification again. We do this in the hope that something, anything, will make us feel in sync with ourselves and the environment as we once were.

THE WORLD WITHIN THE VOID

If the existential age represents our internal experience of the death of God, then our reaction to it is the creation of what is known as *liquid* and *postmodernity*. Post and liquid modernity along with the existential sentiment describe the state of society and culture at the end of the twentieth century and continues for us today.

With the responsibility to fill the void of lost meaning systems placed on our shoulders, we began a flurry of activity and creation to fill the void. We focused on our world and ourselves. We created new products, ideas, and meaning systems. Some of us doubled down on the renaissance humanist project known as the science of "man," trying to find the answers to life deep within our minds and bodies in the hope that we would find the best way to live. Some of us believed that human power could become limitless, if only we could figure ourselves out.

It is not a coincidence that psychology and psychoanalysis emerged around the same time as Nietzsche's famous proclamation of the death of God. We sought the power to understand ourselves, to fix ourselves, to maximize pleasure, and work toward some ideal. Consequently, hundreds of theories of human behaviour were created over the proceeding hundred years. Psychoanalysis, behavioural science, and cognitive-behaviour therapy are all focused on helping us to understand and improve ourselves. We now consume and create new ideas and products in a hunt for existential perfection, but unfortunately, we are insatiable. So we create more and more possibilities to keep up with our own demand. The world becomes full of new gadgets, theories, institutions, and symbols that we hope will permanently satiate our desire for instant gratification. In short, we are trying to create our way out of existential paradox, but this has only led to a confounding postmodern world where we drown in our own creations.

ANYTHING GOES IN OUR POSTMODERN WORLD

The most fundamental aspect of postmodernism is that all knowledge is thought of as relative rather than absolute. There is no grounding, absolute meaning system to anchor our knowledge. This relativism came about through the idea that the interpretation of literature was not objective. Specifically, it was a way of acknowledging different ways one could interpret a text depending on one's background. Thus, there is no "correct" interpretation of any given literary work, just individual views and opinions. Another idea that arose from this is that reality is quite possibly different from our perception of it and that it may not even be within our grasp of understanding. To put it in the words of Richard Tarnas, "there exists a plurality of perspectives through which the world can be interpreted, and there is no authoritative independent criterion according to which one system can be determined to be more valid than others."[77]

So, in this current environment where anything goes, we no longer work toward a single, absolute ideal. Instead, we work toward whatever ideal we believe to be worthwhile to us as individuals. In the absence of a greater, absolute meaning or myth, many of us default to our hunter-gather tendencies that seek the instant gratification of power and pleasure. In this case, our ideal is what we believe will provide us with maximum power and pleasure in today's world. It is this aspect of postmodernity that causes liquid modernity. Where postmodernity refers to the rational understanding of our current world, liquid modernity is how we experience it.

WE ARE ALL LIQUID

Hyper-capitalism, increased globalization, and postmodern relativism converge to create a society that Zygmunt Bauman describes as liquid. A liquid society is one where there is instability in the meanings, categories, and frames of reference that once provided a sense of certainty and coherence. It is a society where knowledge is always in flux and open-ended. In other words, the ideas, beliefs, institutions and ways of being that we once saw as somehow eternal and ironclad are now seen as just choices or "offerings." We no longer have a consistent system of ideals on which we can depend to give our lives meaning, structure, and direction.[78]

The most fundamental example of this is the "bankruptcy" of Christian-based rules for morality that had, for over 1500 years, seeped in and become part of the worldview of Westerners. Even if some Westerners were not historically Christian, Christianity nevertheless, heavily influenced much of Western societies' institutions and cultures. In the nineteenth century and up to today, traditionally Christian rules and ways of being are increasingly challenged by a cacophony of new ideas. However, because there is no other moral code as entrenched as the Christian one, we fill this vacuum with a multitude of quick-fix, superficial, and often conflicting moral-ethical offerings to guide our lives. Bookstores are filled with titles like 10 Rules for a Great Life or Change Your Life in Just 30 Days. While there is nothing inherently "wrong" with such books per se, they often lack the complexity and depth that past religions and spiritualities provided and do not address the underlying existential questions that we humans grapple with.

SO MANY OFFERINGS, SO LITTLE MEANING

There are so many conflicting ideas about how to live a "good" life these days. This is because capitalism, globalization, hyper-connectivity, the democratization of media, and ubiquitous advertising flood our world with offerings at a break-neck speed. This is a flood that erodes the foundation of any solid meaning system we once had, while replacing it with new ones that all promise to maximize our pleasure if we just keep up with the torrent! These offerings can be anything that we consume, from hip new songs, new gadgets, taboo words, and educational trends, to the latest social movements sweeping the nation. They are the things that fill up our time, grab our focus, and give us a momentary sense of importance, security, and pleasure. We drape ourselves in the latest offerings attempting to create a new, solid meaning system in this deluge. The problem is these offerings do not permanently maximize pleasure and minimize pain for us.

There is always something shiny, seductive, and new vying for our attention, so they become disposable. It has become almost a cliché to use the latest smartphone as an example of disposability. Not only do companies churn out a new version a couple of times a year, but they also openly admit that they purposely make old phones obsolete by making them unable to run the latest apps.

This is not just about tech, either. Spirituality has also become as commoditized and disposable as smartphones. We no longer devote the time to fully immerse ourselves in a spiritual path (lest it be the wrong one) so we purchase innumerable quasi-spiritual, out-of-context snippets taken from grand philosophical or religious systems of the past that have been re-packaged into easily digestible step-by-step guides for happiness. Think about the last time you looked at the self-help or spirituality section of your local bookstore or searched those same topics on YouTube. There are not just a few choices like in the past, there are thousands of these quick-fix, self-help messages. Our bookshelves have become a Frankenstein's monster of often-conflicting messages. At the same time, we fear falling behind and missing out on a "better" way to live, so we dispose of these offerings almost as soon as we get them. No doubt spending lots of money along the way.

THE HUNTER-GATHERER IN LIQUID TIMES

"Protect me from what I want" read the art installation in Times Square created in 1982 by the American conceptual artist Jenny Holzer. It was one of her "truisms" that were meant to provoke thought about the human condition via pithy and poignant statements. She was alluding to the fact that it was becoming harder and harder for us to resist our desire for instant gratification in the world that we created. At one time, nature and then God mitigated our desires, but our hunter-gather DNA is no match for liquid times.

The speed, hyper-newness, and disposability of almost everything today directly stimulate our desire for instant pleasure and security, and without absolute spiritual rules or nature to stop us from gorging, it is almost impossible to resist. This new way of being also distracts us from perusing deep contemplation about our lives and our place in the universe. Everything around us is insecure and disposable yet promises security and an absolute solution. When we view something as disposable, it does not hold our attention or satisfy us for long. As a result of our whole lives being filled with disposable offerings, we feel empty and powerless. Nothing we hold onto holds any weight. They are like ghosts of meaning and purpose.

THE NEED FOR SPEED (OF CONSUMPTION)

The abundance and disposability of offerings lead to the need for speed and agility of consumption, lest we miss out on something truly solid and lastingly meaningful. In liquid times humans are led by the drive for ever-increasing seductive offerings that are being produced faster than they can be consumed. Bauman writes that,

> speed, movement, and being "light on one's feet" are viewed as the most efficient ways to live with satisfaction in liquid times. Moreover, in liquid times where "salvation seekers are advised to move quickly enough not to risk over testing any spot's endurance learn that...walking is better than sitting, running is better than walking and surfing is better yet than running.[79]

Quite appropriately, especially given our hunter-gatherer DNA, Bauman suggests that humans have become like game hunters whose sole task is to continuously pursue "kills" and "fill our game bags to capacity" with offerings.[80] We do this in anticipation of finally finding that perfect idea or thing that may last for longer or give us that edge in self-esteem and security. But just like it was for our hunter-gatherer ancestors, the hunt can be just as thrilling as the kill. The pursuit of offerings turns into a compulsion and each successive hunt and kill makes us more obsessed with the hunt itself. We are always looking over our shoulder for the next new and shiny offering that promises more power or pleasure because the satiation never lasts.

Thus, like hunters starving and desperate for a satisfying meal, we gorge on, and then discard the carcasses of used offerings, feel the disappointment of broken promises, and head off to start the hunt anew. Dumps filled with electronics, or discount bins of spiritual self-help books will be the midden piles of our society, proving that all these seductive offerings fell short and that we must continue the search, each time with greater urgency. So, the corporations exploit our dissatisfaction with our liquid existence. Our need to reconcile the excess of unsatisfying offerings with our desire for a meaningful purpose results in an "existential vertigo" that sends us scurrying faster than ever before.

As the choice, speed, and disposability of offerings increase, so do our expectations for pleasure, security, and power. Instead of relying on a personal meaning system to guide us, we hunt for offerings that promise the surest way to tranquility. Inevitably, this leads us to try out different meanings as fast as possible. God forbid we run out of time before discovering the perfect one! Meaning and purpose become like speed-dating or a kind of meaning-tourism. At the same time, disposability feels good to us because it taps into our genetic need for novelty and excitement.

We cling to our "cult of novelty" so much so that anything that stands in the way of progress is viewed as a hindrance to humanity and even evil.

Liquid modernity is like salt on the wound of existential realities that have been recently exposed by the eroding of our old comforts and meaning systems. The knowledge of our finitude makes finding the "right" path a matter of urgency. It is no wonder that for the human in liquid times, the anxiety caused by the need to find a stable meaning can become debilitating and paralyzing. That is, as we realize that the offerings for meaning fall short, it is inevitable that we become filled with anxiety and dread. In this way, existential paradox, the realization that we cannot achieve the perfect bliss we have the capability of imagining, is exacerbated and we reach for those seductive offerings to allay that dread. The freedom of choice in an excess of offerings leads Bauman to conclude that:

> this society of ours is a society of consumers, and just as the rest of the world as-seen-and-lived by consumers, culture [and meaning systems] turns into a warehouse of meant-for-consumption products—each vying for the shifting/drifting attention of prospective consumers in the hope to attract it and hold it for a bit longer than a fleeting moment.[81]

NEOLIBERALISM: OUR RESPONSIBILITY TO PRODUCE AND CONSUME

Neoliberalism is the inevitable consequence of transferring the responsibility for maximizing pleasure and security to each of us as individuals. It is a natural development of the Ubermensch concept. It is not necessarily that an evil group of Mr. Burns' type Illuminati came up with this diabolical concept to enslave us all, but rather that our need to produce and consume in the modern world has led to the next level of capitalism that some people in corporations and government have exploited and weaponized for their own profit, power, and pleasure.

Neoliberalism refers to the economization of life to ensure that everything in society and each of us as individuals is the most efficient agent of capitalism as possible.[82] It is the natural consequence of our lives becoming primarily about consuming as many seductive offerings as possible, and in turn, becoming offerings ourselves. Neoliberalism tells us that we should not only value more and immediate pleasure over grand meaning but also that we are solely responsible to make sure we get it.

This means that, as agents of capitalism, we maximize our buying, consuming, and producing potential while, at the same time, ensuring we do not become a burden on the system. In the resulting zeitgeist, everything in society is viewed through an economic lens, including us humans who become *Homo economicus,* a being primarily focused on making money, consuming, and producing, rather than *Homo sapiens* who contemplate and question their existence. But rather than the government or companies directly trying to coerce us, we are often complicit in participating in our own self-surveillance and enforcement of this agenda. This is not because we consciously want to, but because we are guided by our desires to maximize pleasure in the absence of a sustainable meaning system.

Michele Foucault calls this *governmentality* or self-governance and it is how we normalize our trajectory toward becoming efficient consumers.[83] We work towards getting closer and closer to an ideal that is not our own and that is heavily influenced by the capitalist ideal. Toxic productivity or compulsive busyness, then, is at least partially our internalization of this agenda since productivity often benefits companies, businesses, and organizations more than it benefits us. Yet, it is difficult not to buy into it. Even though we burn ourselves out, develop anxiety, or become depressed, our belief that we must continuously produce and consume in support of the system keeps us going. Our perceived reward is that elusive offering that will finally bring us deep, meaningful fulfillment.

Crises of meaning and mental health are generally considered to be negative for humanity, but mental illness is good from a capitalist perspective so long as we buy the pills or other solutions that can keep us consuming and producing. Government and business sanctioned therapy is often based on a medical model of mental health interventions that promote medicating the problem rather than getting to the root of it. If the government or company cannot monetize the therapy that we prefer, then we have to pay for it out of our own pocket. Another example of the narrow neoliberal perspective is how the Trans Mountain Pipeline, as part of their application to Canada's National Energy Board, espoused the economic benefits of a potential oil spill![84] In today's world, as long as something can be monetized, it is seen as good.

Our internalization and normalization of the neoliberal ideal have a significant effect on our experience of meaning and purpose. It plays into our need for security. Ernest Becker argued that our main driver is the maintenance of self-esteem. This refers to how much power we think we have over our own environment.[85] Since neoliberalism and liquid modernity create a sense of insecurity and scarcity, we exist in a state of constant uncertainty that we hope will be soothed by being even more productive or consuming more things. We also tend to couple our meaning and purpose with the way we make money because we find it difficult to separate our personal needs from these powerful neoliberal forces. We feel uneasy if we devote time and energy to something that does not at least have the potential to make money. We fear the loss of security, falling behind, and missing out. In fact, the toxic narratives of progress and toxic productivity have also influenced our attitude toward play. Today, we feel guilty and lazy if we spend too much time in leisure. One of the most toxic yet prevalent attitudes these days is summed up in the phrase "I'll sleep when I'm dead." What neoliberal and nihilistic brainwashing!

DISENTANGLING OURSELVES FROM THE EXPECTATIONS OF THE WORLD

While it is true that our hunter-gatherer DNA seeks novelty, excitement, and instant gratification, it is not necessarily our fault in the modern world if addiction to drugs, alcohol, food, or sex enters our lives. Our sense of self has become chained to the neoliberal agenda, and when things go sideways in life as a result of systemic forces, there is no recognition of the failures of the system, and instead, the individual is considered solely responsible and even blamed for the condition of their life.

There is an expectation in the neoliberal society that each of us should be forming ourselves into the ideal form of human for the capitalist system. That is, we should be someone who consumes and produces as much as possible. At the same time, we are not to burden the system with the problems that develop as a result of our loyalty to it. If we are unable to fit into this mold, it is not necessarily the state that corrects our behaviour, but we ourselves, through the internalized expectations and norms of the system. Thus, if we are unable to successfully fulfill the neoliberal agenda of producing and consuming, we are taught that we are the problem. But, I hope you have picked up throughout this book that we do not really stand that much of a chance against the expectations of this system. As Yuval Harari says and as we have seen throughout this book, our expectations of life are crucial to life satisfaction.[86] Thus, to have a fighting chance for a meaningful life, we need to disentangle our meaning from the expectations of our mismatched, liquid, and neoliberal world. The problem is that we have internalized neoliberal expectations into our views of ourselves and thus, even if our meaning is not directly economic in nature, it is likely that hyper-capitalist ideals are embedded in our decisions and how we live them out.

An essential part of externalizing expectations requires knowing that our current culture has made us addicted to novelty and excitement to such a degree that our expectations for our self-created meaning systems are much too high. If we do not find a purpose that gives us a psychological high, then we think there is something wrong with us because we cannot find our passion. We humans cannot self-create the same level of meaning system that nature provided our paleo-ancestors, but we keep trying to.

YOU MUST CHOOSE, BUT CHOOSE WISELY

These days, we feel our meaning is our own to choose. We feel we must decide the best way to maximize pleasure in our lives, but we also try desperately to avoid this responsibility. In a grand reversal of what many believed about liberty at the beginning of the modern era, Jean-Paul Sartre professed that humans were actually condemned to be free and that we alone were responsible for creating the life that we wanted.[87] The sheer amount of choice or offerings that we have in what we can do with our time has never been greater. This abundance of choice sounds like something good, and there is no doubt it has positives. But the burden of freedom and responsibility in this excess of offerings exacerbates the existential anxiety that Sartre wrote so much about. The responsibility to make the best choice to ensure security and pleasure—a worthy meaning and purpose to match our grand visions—is daunting.

On top of all the choices, many of us can no longer rely on an absolute god to guide our decisions because increasing numbers of us are either agnostics or atheists. We each also have some sort of worldview that guides us in our forward movement, whether it is the advice of our parents or the values of our culture. There is a myriad of things that we rely on to make decisions. In liquid modernity, there are many advice offerings, but we can never really know if the choices we make are the best ones. Nevertheless, some of us do mental calculus to try to figure out the perfect choice. Some of us think that if we research enough and learn enough we will eventually come to an irrefutable conclusion. So, trying to figure out what to do with our time and lives often becomes a burdensome and stressful time-filler. Is this not often what late-night surfing on the internet is all about?

In fact, I would argue that the most obvious consequence of liquid modernity on meaning and purpose is the sheer amount of choice that we have, not just in what we do with our lives, but also in who we want to be—our identity.

One day, a group of us went over to a friend's apartment. We walked in and instantly felt a sense of oppression and heaviness. His walls were completely covered with hundreds of hand-written quotes on paper, all fluttering and jostling for attention in the air conditioning. The quotes ranged in sources from literature and philosophy to business and science, all giving some sort of life advice or view of the world. Some sort of direction for any aspect of life that one could think of. The physical accumulation of these quotes was his attempt to feel grounded within a kaleidoscope of views and perspectives. But the quotes were often contradictory, and he did not dwell on any one of them long enough to let them become meaningfully embodied. Hundreds of contradictory voices screaming for his attention. There were just too many of them to provide any sort of direction at all. As soon as you gaze upon a quote that gives you comfort and direction for a moment, the next one gets blown by the air conditioning drawing you in and giving you a completely different view.

With social media, the bombardment of perspectives and ideas is taken to a dizzying level. People post all sorts of often-contradictory views and ideas in an attempt to lessen the deep anxiety and dread they feel. But because we all need to stay light on our feet, we have to quickly search out the next one before we have a chance to contemplate the one we just posted. It is our frantic attempt to find something to guide our lives. Alas, there are just too many options vying for our attention, and none of them seem quite right.

HEAVEN ON EARTH

Meaning in liquid times is mired by comparison and expectations like no other time in human history. Heaven is no longer the realm of God, but the perceived lifestyles of celebrities and social media influencers projected onto our brains by liquid media, making us strive for lives that are just as imaginary as heaven was. Just like we downloaded God's responsibility onto our shoulders, so too did we download the existential perfectionism of heaven. Because heaven does not exist for many of us anymore, media and social media have become our guides for what we should be pursuing in life—the new "heaven on Earth" to work toward.

For many of us, especially in industrialized countries, it is not enough anymore to have a middle-class income and lifestyle. We must live our "best lives" that we now believe is a birthright, and the new prevailing meaning system. Most of us base this idealized life on social media, so we go about pursuing those things. When we do not achieve this grand vision or cannot come up with a vision to pursue, we get upset, anxious, and depressed.

So, what was once the exception for most of us has now become a very dangerous expectation. Unrealistic expectations breed unhappiness. On top of this, with social media and hyper-connectivity, there are now hyper-comparisons and hyper-"keeping up with the Joneses." It is not necessarily all about the accumulation of money and power either. We now see millennials quitting their jobs, buying a homestead, living van-life, and documenting their lives on YouTube, and with the magic of editing, portraying a near perfect existence. This social media curation is like the heaven of old because it seems to communicate that if we follow a specific path, near-perfect happiness, tranquility, and meaning are possible. While this is not new, it has become extreme in liquid times.

FUTURIZATION: LIVING FOR TOMORROW

Our freedom to choose and the need to keep up with our imagined ideal have pushed our goals so far into the future that we are almost always living in anticipation of the future and just tolerating the present. Striving for a time in our lives when we can finally feel secure is arduous and painful. First, we are in school, then we work our way up in a company, or spend our time trying to figure out what to do with our lives.

For many of us, the present has become boring and meaningless, so we pin our hopes for satisfaction on some future time because meaning has conceptually become profoundly linear and future-focused. The pleasure and security we seek are far off and our gratification is extremely delayed. When the day comes when we can retire, or buy that expensive car, our satisfaction is short-lived, so we fill our time with more disposable thrills that, themselves, become our whole lives. Satisfaction and security become elusive once again, and the present is either boring or loaded with time-filling distractions. In essence, the present has now also become disposable and anticipation for the future is valued more than what is happening now. Unfortunately, the future only exists in our imagination.

EXISTENCE BEYOND SURVIVAL: A PROBLEM OF MEANING

Our survival instincts are just that. They are only meant for survival no matter how our modern minds try to story them. The mismatch between our lifestyles and our instincts is part of the reason many of us feel existential paradox down to our bones these days. Nothing quite satisfies us for long because we are living way beyond survival, yet we have the same survival mechanisms guiding our lives. Parts of our DNA no longer seem to work in our favour because, as a species, we are not adapted to this new environment. That is, our factory model, hunter-gatherer DNA is outdated and not quite conducive to life satisfaction in the modern world we have created.

Meaning for our Paleolithic ancestors was directed at something very important—survival. Our pleasure, excitement, and novelty-seeking DNA was singularly and continuously focused on keeping us alive and aligned with what we saw happening in the natural world. And even though in the Neolithic era we lived a life less driven by survival than the hunter-gatherers, survival was still at the forefront of our minds compared to today. So, we are so far removed from our baseline existence that our pleasure-seeking DNA is not a requirement for how we live. We do not need to be fighting for physical survival every day, yet our inclination to gorge still exists for food and all the seductive offerings available. In a sense, this aspect of our DNA is almost like our appendix or wisdom teeth, something of a bygone era that we no longer really need but is still very much part of our genetic make-up.

Because for most of us in industrialized areas our basic survival is guaranteed, we now must find a way to convince ourselves that what we choose to do with our lives is of the utmost importance. This can lead to renewed absolutism.

Biologically, we are not really meant to do more than just guarantee our survival, so after survival needs are met, our existence becomes a bit of a problem to figure out. We hoard experiences, food, and money, convincing ourselves they are necessary. We try to mimic the hunt, but eventually, we get diminishing returns on satisfaction. Then we ask, "now what?" "What is the bigger meaning or myth to participate in?" Then nihilism sets in again.

In his *Book of Disquiet*, Fernando Pessoa perfectly sums up this experience when he writes, "tedium is not the disease of being bored because there is nothing to do, but the more serious disease of feeling that there is nothing worthwhile to do."[88] We want to be certain that what we are doing is of great importance. In our world today, there is certainly a lot to do and fill our time with, but most of it is not worthwhile in terms of physical survival. However, we are now met with the difficult task of convincing ourselves that our activities are worthwhile. And the further we get away from our baseline way of being, the more prone we are to the painful experiences of boredom and meaninglessness. To lessen this pain, our entire lives have become about time-filling, busyness, distraction, and the consumption of offerings.

PROFOUND BOREDOM: THE MAINTENANCE OF OUR LIVES

The modern human condition is largely post-survivalist in nature. We are the only animal on this planet that must figure out what to do with our time because our survival has been assured. Further, as our survival, existence, and lifespans increase, I cannot help but think our boredom will as well, especially as survival becomes easier with every new "progression."

In fact, Lars Svendsen says that once our survival is guaranteed, we lapse into boredom.[89] In the same vein, Viktor Frankl said that beyond survival, we must find a reason for being in this world and something else to do besides survival and pursuing direct pleasure.[90] But because there is no sustainable meaning system or myth, we create, consume, and dig ourselves deeper and deeper into the void of profound boredom.

The speed and disposability of most offerings in liquid times exacerbate this post-survivalist boredom. Every time we create some time-saving device, it just leaves us with higher expectations for how to fill our time, so we fill it with even more time-saving devices to fill the time we created. But alas, the speed, disposability, and unimportance of most of what we fill our lives with just leads to more boredom and meaninglessness. It is an endless feedback loop of trying to satiate our desires by consumption and creation yet creating more and higher expectations in the process. Even as we gorge on the latest seductive offering, we also have one wandering eye looking toward new offerings as they rush past us in our few seconds of respite. Lured by the promise of more, we have already lost interest in what is right in front of us. In liquid times, we also tend to get more bored of our chosen meanings much faster than in the past, or at least, we see them as something that can be exchanged when it no longer excites us.

Hence, meaning is focused on filling our time with the best distraction from this profound boredom rather than finding something of grand importance and significance. As a result, we fall for seductive offerings very easily. It is difficult to find something truly important to us to work towards, but at the same time, we need to fill our time with activity because our "moving" DNA tells us to. This is especially true in midlife. For the first half of our lives, our meaning is dedicated to securing ourselves—a worthwhile goal for sure, and one that occupies us for years. Education, job, marriage, kids, and house. But once all this is achieved, maintenance is boring.

THE TWENTY-FIRST CENTURY: HUMANITY'S COLLECTIVE MIDLIFE CRISIS

In addition, how we go about building this security is often based on childhood complexes, the patterns of behaviour we internalized as a way of dealing with the insecurities of our upbringing. A childhood full of illness may unconsciously push us to become medical doctors and a past of living in poverty may give us the overwhelming desire to be rich at all costs. All of us have these often-unconscious patterns of behaviour that govern how we seek security in our lives, but once we achieve that security, or over-come that childhood pattern, we need something new to guide and engage us. It is often at this point that we experience midlife crises, except that nowadays, this type of crisis does not just occur in midlife. It happens whenever we realize that the default meaning passed on to us through culture does not provide the satisfaction we were told it would, and when we realize our survival and security are assured so that more of anything will not satisfy us. For some of us, upgrading our homes is not a need for more space, but an expression of our innate need for continued movement and a symbolic chase to break the mundaneness of our mainte-nance-style lives.

At this point of realization, we can choose to continue with the default path we were on, or question the meaning system of the first half of our lives, make a U-turn, and go back and figure out what was meaningful to us before we got caught up in the cul-turally dominant ways of living. In his book, *Finding Meaning in the Second Half of Life*, James Hollis tells us to go back to our childhood for clues about what really excited us.[91] We can see this as a metaphor for humanity overall. Now that we, as humans, have reached a stage when physical survival is guaranteed and most of us are not satisfied with the spiritual systems of the past, do we look back to our childhood to see how we should be spending our time? Perhaps as a species we are experiencing a collective midlife crisis.

Remember the Ubermensch? It represents the power and freedom to create our world and lives how we want to. But this myth is faltering. Now the Ubermensch is fat, sick, narcissistic, indebted, and nearly dead. We, ourselves, have become the problem—human vs. ourselves. We have become addicted to the sweet pleasures of all the seductive offerings, and just as an addict's hunt for their drug of choice takes over their whole lives, our society is taken over by our cravings for instant excitement, novelty, pleasure, power, and excess, from the new smartphone to latest social movement. When we do not have a constant stream before our eyes and in our minds, we get depressed and anxious. In the spaces between our consumption, we feel that something is very wrong with our lives, yet even in the presence of so much to do, see, and have, we become easily bored. So, the Ubermensch has become another illusion of human progress. Rather than making us feel more in sync with life by reconciling existential paradox, it has made our relentless search for meaning and purpose far more difficult.

DOUBLING DOWN: DISTRACTION AND SEDATION

We deal with the nagging pain of existential paradox through distraction and sedation, or what Berman calls "dullardism." This is a combination of distraction and sticking our head in the sand, "going unconscious by means of a (steady stream of) tranquilizers, alcohol, TV, spectator sports...compulsive busyness and workaholism."[92] We are swept away by the seductive flow of liquid times, allowing the latest offerings to lull us into a trance where existential paradox and crisis are masked. We are "quick on our feet" in consuming all the latest offerings without stopping to reflect—we are immersed in the continuous change and movement that our DNA loves; where everything is perpetually new.

Our lives are guided by the prevailing standards and norms of our time, which are heavily influenced by consumerism and capitalism. We are told by the media and advertising around us what we want, who we are, and what we should do—the new myth. Soren Kierkegaard named this type of person the "automatic cultural" person. This is a person who automatically and uncritically accepts all the messages that are fed to them.[93] In this category, there are innumerable automatic meanings to which one can dedicate their life. This approach to life means never having to think about one's meaning and purpose, but just going through the culturally accepted motions of getting a job, getting married, having kids, watching a whole lot of sports, retiring at 65, and then babysitting grandkids. Throughout all of these stages, we are seduced by offerings of all types. If we begin to feel the inoculation wearing off, we just pray harder to the "neon god we made" by getting a bigger TV, going on a grander vacation, or getting a newer and bigger house.[3] We loyally live out the meaning and purpose they are selling us.

All of us watch TV, relax, and do many of the things that Berman characterizes as dullardism, but that does not make us all dullards. The difference is the level of awareness of why we do the things we do and whether or not we allow automatic decision-making to lull us into a space of passive conformity where we no longer question what is going on around us.

DOUBLING BACK: RETURNING TO THE ABSOLUTE

For some of us, meaning is about seeking that perfect and irrefutable solution—a return to something absolute. The irony is that the relativism of our modern era makes us crave the absolutes of yore more than ever before. In our world, it is hard to convince our brains that such an absolute exists. Yet, to ease our fears and anxiety, we need an absolute meaning system that proclaims to be the one true meaning and purpose.

---

3   This is part of the lyrics "And the people bowed and prayed to the neon god they made" from Simon and Garfunkel's Sound of Silence.

However, in liquid times there are so many competing views that are not easily explained away. In the presence of so many offerings, we feel threatened and go to great lengths to protect the certainty of our meaning systems. So we must denigrate and dehumanize them. One of the main tenets of *terror management theory* is that individuals and societies will protect their meaning systems from perceived outside threats using extreme measures.[94] Whether it is religious fundamentalists, anti-abortion crusaders, or New Age fanatics, all need to prove at all costs that their meaning system is correct. However, this rigidity leads to fragility.

This is not just reserved for the religious, but for any of us who hold onto a belief system, like political ideologies and even psychological theories, to explain our world. I was recently in a presentation that purported that nearly all negative behaviours that humans exhibit can be attributed to some past traumatic event in our lives. While I will not go into why I find this an overly simplified view of human behaviour, it is an example of how absolutism reduces our world to black and white or good and evil, and once we label something as evil, it becomes something to crusade against for our own sense of security.

Morris Berman explains this *derapage* as when we take a relatively simple system that is not meant to encompass all of reality and then proceed, nevertheless, to "map that truth on all of reality."[95]

After that, we reject or denigrate any form of disagreement and build our entire world or career around this new simplified system of belief.

Thus, the very act of convincing ourselves that our meaning system is absolute becomes a full-time task that we feel is worthwhile to dedicate our lives to. Absolutism is the belief that what we are doing with our lives is of the utmost importance and irrefutable. At the same time, it provides us with the comfort of having clear, concrete answers while the storm of liquid modernity is whirling around us. It gives us a sense of power and security because we believe we are the special, privileged ones in possession of the "truth." If doubt creeps in, we just pray harder and double down on our own beliefs. This is effective for keeping a crisis of meaning at bay, at least for a while. However, as we have seen throughout history, the fight to preserve absolute beliefs has only led to division, violence, and destruction.

The attempt to use our limited knowledge and power to create a heaven on Earth has backfired. We can instantly gratify ourselves at any moment, but it has made us sick. We can delay our gratification far into the future, but that has made us anxious, depressed and violent. So, what do we do now?

"The great spirit made time and space elusive to humans."[96]
— *Ed McGaa,* Nature's Way: Native Wisdom for Living in
Balance with the Earth.

*"We are challenged with an unprecedented task, and
the task is to develop an art, to develop an art to living
with permanent uncertainty."*[97]
— *Zygmunt Bauman,* The Trouble With Being Human

Chapter 5
A NEW MYTH OF BEING

THE PROBLEM

We are searching souls within the "stuckness" of the human condition in liquid times—the desire for desires, as Tolstoy said. What is needed now is a sustainable myth based on something worthwhile, something that is not about the direct pursuit of pleasure. The question is, how can we move away from the current myth based on producing and consuming and, at the same time, avoid going back to one based on delayed gratification for a future time?

THE CHALLENGE

The most important challenge for the human species today is to not lose sight of the fact that we seek survival and pleasure and are also aware of the mysterious nature of our very existence. We know the universe and everything within it exists, but we have no idea why. Like Becker says, "beyond the absurdity of one's own life, beyond the human viewpoint…is the fact of the tremendous creative energies of the cosmos that are using us for some purpose we don't know."[98]

While we have learned much about the human condition through our collective journey and celebrated many false victories along the way, we always run the risk of falling back into either absolutism or the hedonistic nihilism of liquid times. Thus, moving forward, we must avoid what Martin Heidegger called "forgetfulness of being."[99] In other words, we must not get caught up in the seduction of liquid times and, instead continue to think deeply about our existence. Our existential enlightenment can easily slip away while living in the compulsive busyness of the world. Therefore, living in the world today requires remaining "mindful of being."[4] However, we cannot do this without a myth that will infuse our struggle with meaning and significance. What would this new myth look like?

---

4   Forgetfulness of being and mindfulness of being are Martin Heidegger's terms from his 1927 *Being and Time.*

Our new myth would not be fleeting and disposable. It would provide us with our instant gratification, yet reign in our potentially destructive desires like nature and God once did. It would be powerful enough to re-enchant our world, make us feel a part of something bigger, and also help us to recognize our limitations so that we do not let hubris lead us to another false victory. This is the myth we need to work towards.

THE FOUNDATION

Within Joseph Campbell's hero's journey monomyth[5] is the notion that a hero returning from their journey, who has gone through the ordeal and road of trials, has learned to become "the master of two worlds." Becoming master of two worlds finally allows the hero the strength to live in the ordinary world. Being a master of two worlds gives the hero the ability to hold together all aspects of existence that they have learned along the way. In the monomyth, this ability is the magical power or elixir that makes them a leader or saviour in the ordinary world. The hero's challenge when crossing back into the ordinary world is to maintain a "cosmic" standpoint when faced with earthly joy, pain, and knowledge. This represents

---

5   The hero's journey monomyth is the name Joseph Campbell gives to the universal themes, structures, and plots found especially in humanity's myths of spiritual growth and enlightenment, but also in any story of change or growth. The ordeal, road of trials, ordinary world, and master of two worlds are some of the seventeen stages that a hero must go through to achieve "enlightenment."

our final challenge, too. Thus, we must explore what being "master of two worlds" means for us today.

If we are to examine future myths for their sustainability, at the very least, it would be prudent to examine them using the functions of a myth as defined by Joseph Campbell: the mystical, the cosmological, and the socio-ethical.

THE MYSTICAL: LIVING IN AWE AND ACCEPTANCE

A sustainable myth must satisfy certain levels or functions of existence. It must offer a map of how we should conduct all aspects of our lives. There needs to be an acknowledgment of the mystical aspect of life to ground us in the idea that the universe is ultimately mysterious and unknowable.[100] But the question is how can we address this mystical part of life without resorting to absolutes? At this point, we cannot go back to the Paleolithic era, the dogmatic religions, nor can we continue to rely on today's nihilistic hedonism. As Camus stresses, we cannot look to the past for solutions:

Such are the "returns" to the middle ages, to a primitive mentality, to the so-called "natural life," to religion—in short, to the arsenal of old solutions. But to give a shadow of usefulness to these cures, several centuries' contributions must be denied; we must pretend to be ignorant of what we know very well, to pretend we have learnt nothing, and to efface what is ineffaceable. This is impossible.[101]

Impossible indeed. Camus himself admitted that even if there is a cosmic order or God, we cannot ever fully understand it. So, we should not try to create and impose systems of meaning on the universe and world. Consequently, in living life, "there is nothing on which to hang a mythology, a literature, an ethic or a religion; only stones, stars and those truths which the hand can touch."[102] However, we humans still have a deep need to find somewhere to hang our beliefs, so why not make the foundation the mystery and uncertainty of life itself? Some new existentialists are trying to do just that.

Modern-day existentialist Kirk Schneider suggests that humans should develop an *enchanted agnostic* disposition toward the mystery of the universe that falls somewhere between nihilism and absolute religion.[103] We can develop this disposition by being *in awe* of the mystery. Awe is our fundamental experience of the mystery of existence that is the "humility and wonder, thrill and anxiety of living—and the capacity to be moved."[104] Awe is when we fully accept the paradox, ambiguity, and absurdity of the human condition while keeping in mind our place within the cosmic mystery. It is a heightened consciousness that helps us to realize and prioritize the profoundness in which our consciousness resides and that is present all around us.[105]

Alan Watts suggested that part of the reason many Buddhist monasteries are found atop misty mountains with sweeping and often terrifying vistas is to remind us of our small place in an awesome, mysterious world. The moment the monks wake up, they are reminded of this and it stays with them every moment of the day. They start with the principles of awe, mystery, and vastness, holding this idea to bring about acceptance and to remain lucidly aware that this is as far as humans can go. We should not expect to fully understand our existence in the universe because space and time will forever be elusive to humans. We are *within* an immense system, not gods of it. The awe that comes with allowing the mystery to just be, can bring about beautiful experiences. Exploring the terrors and marvels of existential paradox leads us to aesthetic experiences of awe and tranquility.[106]

The experience of awe in our daily lives overcomes nihilism, dogma, and purposelessness because it helps us to accept that we exist in a mysterious universe and that although we may never come to know it, there must be a reason behind it. However, with conscious acceptance of this mystery, we must also resist the impulse to impose our absolutes onto it when its grandeur incites fear.[107]

But just because we may never be able to fully understand the universe or ourselves, it does not mean that we cannot try. That *is* what we have been doing for thousands of years. Ironically, acknowledging our fundamental limitations as human beings frees us from a lot of angst. For, it is the testing of our limits that is thrilling and that energizes. We need limits to thrive.

So here it is. Our new myth requires that we be in awe of the mystery of existence and accept our limitations. The grand mystery itself is the large-scale meaning system on which we should base our personal meaning. But we still need a template that helps us to concretize, internalize, and live within the mystery. We must wear existential paradox on our sleeves. We need to find a way to make the mystery the foundation of our lives here on Earth.

THE COSMOLOGICAL: LIVING LIKE A REBEL

As humans, we need tangible ways to connect to the mystical aspects of myth in our daily lives. In most organized religions, there are practices designed to remind us of the mysterious. Buddhist temples are built in awe-inspiring places and Christians accept the body and blood of Christ in the form of bread and wine in Holy Communion. These are rituals integrated into our lives intended to attach us to the mystery and remind us of the tenets of their respective religion. But throughout history, this approach has been a slippery slope toward absolutism as we can quickly forget that these practices are designed to remind us of the mystery rather than an absolute truth. We can avoid returning to absolutes yet keep the mystical close to our hearts by becoming what Camus calls *metaphysical rebels.*

Camusian rebellion is the rejection of any absolute or final state of knowledge. It is a constant rebellion against certainties of all kinds whether metaphysical, sociological, or scientific. It is the attitude that fights for uncertainty and ambiguity in as many aspects of life as possible. We challenge and accept our limitations at the same time.

First, we acknowledge that there is no way to fully resolve existential paradox, that no meaning or purpose will provide that ideal state of fullness that we seek, and anyone who tries to tell us otherwise is selling something. The Camusian rebel does not try to fix the human condition or our place in the universe. It is the belief that we have limitations as humans and accepting that aligns us more to the universe. Camus called this *living the absurd life.* Consciously living the absurd life is a way of life that embodies the mystery of being.

A person living as an absurd rebel rejects absolutism and does their best to avoid getting seduced, lulled, and distracted like so many of us today. This person believes that giving into absolutism and sedation is a potentially destructive and unreliable way to live. This person embodies Schneider's enchanted agnostic attitude that lies between nihilism and absolutism. This way of life is not very easy, but the challenge and struggle to live as an absurd rebel becomes something worthwhile to dedicate our lives to. The absurd rebel takes in the tensions and paradoxes of the world but rather than numbing themselves against it with distraction or absolute answers, they confront it. But in confronting life, there still needs to be a way to process it. Camus believes that the act of creation is the best way of living as a rebel in the shadow of the absurd.[108]

As rebels, we are artists working within the limits of our medium and chosen form—the human condition. Our lives become an art form and the goal is to continue to experiment, ideate, and experiment again until our paint runs out. Art itself is the act of taking in the world around us, interacting with it, and then sending forth a unique form of it into the world. It is our way of processing the problems of our existence without denying that they exist, like this book. Absurd art is about creating something while knowing that it will never tell the whole story, nor will it fill the void. It is trying to make sense of the world, but knowing our explanations will always fall short. So we must try again.

True art hovers between failure and perseverance, negation and statement. It is created between detachment and passion. It must maintain the longing, recognize the limits, yet proceed with a steadfast determination within the paradox of the absurd. Thus, the artist lives in a state of ambiguity, incapable of denying the real, yet eternally bound to question it in its eternally unfinished aspects.[109] Art is a way of holding together the two terms of existential paradox—our longing for perfect satiation of our desires with the knowledge of the futility of that longing. It is a way of concretizing the absurd in life.

It is no wonder that Camus equates artistic endeavours to a rebellion that demands unity, but since an ultimate unity cannot be found, a substitute universe is created that temporarily satisfies the quest. Rebellion becomes a way of creating universes, as does art.[110] To become an artist means to accept the call to revolt without end, with the understanding that our creations will not "give any explanations or solutions to the problems of life" but they may help us be little more comfortable with the mystery of life.[111] Thus, turning to art and creation can help us to mitigate our impulse to seek certainty in times of psychological stress.

Of course, living an absurd life does not mean we have to be an artist or reject all meaning. Instead, it is the realization that we should not pursue that feeling of wholeness—it is futile. It is viewing everything, including ourselves, as art. It is the realization that all those seductive offerings of liquid modernity will not fill our soul for long and so we should have an artist's attitude toward life, work, and metaphysical beliefs. Scientists can be thought of as having an artist's attitude when we look at their approach to their work. They recognize patterns and come up with theories of functional "truths," but all the while, they realize their findings are not final. They are only theories that work for now, until new factors shift existing patterns and theories. Thus, they continue to push against the limitations but never accept a final state. They are absurd artists.

Living as an absurd rebel is not easy and never has been. Part of this is because it serves to liberate an individual from a restrictive view of self and the world that is often comfortable and secure. However, if we are to ground ourselves in the awe and mystery of life, it means having the courage to dwell in ideas that are as large as life itself and to view everything as art. Nietzsche, writes, "art and nothing but art . . . we have art in order not to die of truth."[112]

THE SOCIOLOGICAL-ETHICAL: LIVING PRUDENTLY

So where does this bring us? We are flying through the mysterious universe on a spinning rock going who knows where, for who knows what reason, busying ourselves as absurd rebellious artists along the way. But we must still navigate our pleasure-seeking DNA in the modern world.

Balancing pleasure and pain is a very complex task for symbolic, self-reflexive, and future-focused beings in liquid times. But there is a sophisticated philosophical and ethical system by which to do so. One that is based on lifetimes of observations of human nature, and philosophical debate about the good life. One that has passed through rigorous arguments and logic challenges of other philosophers. It gives us a way of thinking about living in this world that is probably closest to our true wild nature. For those of us who are dedicated to the art of living in existential paradox, awe-based Epicureanism may be able to guide us in almost every aspect of our lives. But this would be a new, modern Epicureanism, one that also considers what we have learned about ourselves and the world over the past two millennia since Epicurus and his followers lived.

The philosophical system that Epicurus put forward may provide a guide that is most harmonious with the mysteries of life. It is based on human limitation and managing animal pleasures in civilization and within a mysterious universe. It does not deny our pleasure-seeking nature or our inability to understand our profound context. Not only do Epicureans insist that humans are limited animals that are no nobler than others, but they also believed that the gods (if they exist) have no influence on humans' affairs and that humans should not concern themselves with them or what they do.

Epicurus would have probably told us not to be all that concerned with the mystery of the universe, but to accept it and only draw from it when our self-importance gets the better of us, or if we begin to fall into nihilism. Instead, Epicurus would tell us to focus on the human world and functioning within the limits of our DNA.

Epicurus believed that while our self-reflexivity and rationality could not hope to understand the nature of the universe, it could, with proper education and training, help us to live a good life in our world.

This education was all about learning the best way to maximize pleasure in life while also functioning well in the human world. According to Epicurus, prudence is the essential wisdom used in living a good life. It is described as the "sober reasoning which examines the motives for every choice and avoidance, and that which drives away those opinions resulting in the greatest disturbance of the soul."[113] Living prudently today involves knowledge of existential paradox and knowing which ways of trying to reconcile it are vain. To do this we have to step back from the flood of seductive offerings to examine which ones will lead to net pleasure and what life goals are worthwhile. To be successful at this, deep self-awareness and awareness of the human condition are essential.

Part of this is being able to recognize what Epicurus called "false or empty opinions" That is, things that we think will lead to more pleasure or security, but actually do not.[114] The most obvious example today is all the products we get seduced into buying, thinking that they will lead to more fulfillment and security. Our essential need for survival is one thing, but our wants have no limits and continue to infinity.[115]

In addition, Epicurus tells us to vary our interests as much as possible. This does not mean indulging in seductive offerings. It means prudently choosing a variety of interests that maximize kinesthetic pleasures (pleasures that engage the body and mind) while avoiding becoming bored, or at the opposite end, obsessed with them. It is being "nomadic" with our interests.

Epicurus instructs that sharing our lives with like-minded friends and community is one of the best ways to ensure the maximization of pleasure, not unlike paleo-human groups of foragers and hunters. Epicurus goes as far as to say that friendship and community may be the most important way of ensuring pleasure and security in our lives.

However, it is not as if meaning is just about managing pleasure. We must participate in the world, but everything we do needs to be evaluated using the practical wisdom of prudence. In life, we have personal goals, but they need to be underpinned by the awareness that, in the end, our goal is net pleasure, not continuous procurement of objects full of empty promises of lasting pleasure or power. The Epicureans knew that fighting for honour and justice was necessary, not only to increase pleasure for others but also for ourselves. So ideally, we would choose life projects that would maximize pleasure and security for friends, family, community, and ourselves.

Combining Epicureanism, Camusian rebellion, and the experience of awe gives us a way to move forward in our modern world that does not lead us back to absolutes or sedation. It helps us to navigate both our pleasure-seeking DNA and our ability to think deeply about life and our universe. And perhaps most important of all, it gives us a new mythical foundation for sustainable meaning and purpose.

FINAL THOUGHTS:
OUR FIGHT, OUR STORY

It is uniquely fitting and serendipitous that I should end this journey with Camus' great existential novel, *The Plague*, a story of how the townspeople of Oran react to a great plague that seals off their town from the rest of the world, stripping their institutions and lives of the meanings and purposes they thought were immutable. Each character struggles to make sense of and find meaning in the plague. In the end, the plague brings them together in solidarity and helps them to realize new meanings and new ways of being as they move forward together.

We finish with this not only because Camus has guided us so much already, or because most of this book has been written during the Covid-19 pandemic, but because the plague is symbolic of existential paradox in our lives and can help us thrive while living with the uncertainty and ambiguity that it brings. The last lines of the novel, when the town is celebrating the end of the plague and crisis are fitting for us:

> And indeed, as he listened to the cries of joy rising from the town, Rieux remembered that such joy is always imperiled. He knew what those jubilant crowds did not know but could have learned from books: that the plague bacillus never dies or disappears for good; that it can lay dormant for years and years in furniture and in linen chests; that it bides its time in bedrooms, cellars and trunks and bookshelves; and perhaps the day would come when, for the bane and enlightening of men, it roused up its rats again and sent them forth to die in a happy city.[116]

The message? Existential paradox, our symbolic plague, strips us down but then creates new meanings and purposes for us as individuals and as a collective. It forces us to do and see things differently. It gives us new directions to go in. It reminds us that there will always be something to fight against and new crusades to engage in. While it may sometimes be sitting dormant, at any moment it can unleash feelings of doubt and dread, and strip us again of what we thought was our meaning and purpose. But this same force will forever keep us in action, creation, and rebellion.

The irony is that every time we feel we are overcoming existential paradox, finally defeating the plague, whether it is by eradicating poverty or disease, ridding ourselves of the problem of death, or inequality, or inventing new myths, we learn that the gulf that separates us from that reconciliation is wider than we believed. Yet, it is this same gulf that makes us creative, imaginative, tenacious, and adaptive. And even if we eventually become gods who can experience any pleasure and power that we want, we will still need to find something worthwhile to do. For as long as there is something in the universe that is unknown, unexplored, or there is a longing for something new, it will pique our hunter-gatherer DNA and propel us off into some unknown direction. The universe requires movement, and no matter how hard we try, we will never be still. This is our fate. And so, the existential paradox that we are so scared of, and that we have even called a plague on our soul, is fundamental to being human.

There is no final answer, just more exploring to do. With this, I will once again lean on Camus' Rieux for some final wisdom on what to do with what seems to be our perennial situation:

He knew that the tale he had to tell could not be one of final victory. It could only be a record of what had to be done and what assuredly would have to be done again in a never ending fight against terror and its relentless onslaughts, despite their personal afflictions, by all who, while unable to be saints but refusing to bow down to pestilences, strive their utmost to be healers.[117]

We must understand how we got to where we are today if we are to be healers of our world, each other, and ourselves. And because we humans make sense of our world and find solidarity through stories, it is our collective story as a species that will help us now. The greatest story of all, our fight for a meaningful existence, is the story of our struggle against our great antagonist and nemesis, existential paradox. That unrequited desire for a sustainable meaning system, for certainty, for a direction that will guide us to unencumbered pleasure and complete security. This is what really drives us, what always has, and what always will.

It is the mysterious cosmic trickster character, ubiquitous throughout world mythology that is deceptive, elusive, and illusory, and makes us strive for existential perfection and then laughs at us when we fail. It is this cycle of trickery, challenge, and failure that keeps us changing, adapting, and shape shifting, and just when we think that we have life pinned down again, it swoops in and strips us of what we thought we knew. It enlightens us. It brings us pain, disappointment, and longing, but it also brings hope, pleasure, and excitement. It is what makes us human, and perhaps most fundamental of all, what keeps us moving along with the flow of the mysterious universe to an unknowable destination because "the wandering life is just too deep a part of our genetic memory for us to forget it completely."[118] But now we must wander in our mysterious universe together, with the full awareness that it is existential paradox itself that gives us our purpose and a fighting chance for a meaningful existence.

ENDNOTES

1   https://cmha.ca/brochure/fast-facts-about-mental-illness/

2   Irvin Yalom, *Existential Psychotherapy* (New York: Basic Books, 1980).

3   Viktor Frankl, *The Will to Meaning* (New York: New American Library Inc, 1969), 68

4   Ibid.

5   Carl Jung, *The Practice of Psychotherapy: Essays on the Psychology of the Transference and Other Subjects* (New York: Pantheon Books, 1954), 83.

6   Irvin Yalom, *Existential Psychotherapy* (New York: Basic Books, 1980), 459.

7   Robert Burton, *Anatomy of Melancholy*, ed. Jackson Holbrook (London: Rowman and Littlefield, 1975), 71.

8   Erich Fromm, *To Have or To Be* (New York: Bloomsbury, 2013/1976), 22.

9   John Cooper, *Pursuits of Wisdom: Six Ways of Life in Ancient Philosophy from Socrates to Plotinus* (Princeton, NJ: Princeton University Press, 2012)

10   Richard Tarnas, *Passion of the Western Mind: Understanding the Ideas That Have Shaped Our Worldview* (New York: Ballantine Books, 1993), 59.

11   Allan Watts, *What is Tao?* (Novato, CA: New World Library, 2001), 37.

12   M. Monier-Williams, *English Sanskrit Dictionary* (London: Kessinger Publications, 2006).

13   Yoshiharu Nakagawa, *Education for Awakening: An Eastern Approach to Holistic Education* (Toronto: University of Toronto Press, 2000), 106; 367.

14   Carl Jung, *The Archetypes and the Collective Unconscious,* 2nd ed., trans. R.F.C. Hull (New York: Bollingdon Foundation Inc., and Princeton University Press, 1990).

15   Sarah Bakewell, *At the Existentialist Café: Freedom, Being and Apricot Cocktails* (New York: Other Press, 2016).

16   Marcus Tellius Cicero, *On Living and Dying Well* (London: Penguin Books, trans. 2012)

17   John Cooper, *Pursuits of Wisdom: Six Ways of Life in Ancient Philosophy from Socrates to Plotinus* (Princeton, NJ: Princeton University Press, 2012)

18   Ibid.

19   Jonathan Yahalom, "Freud and Epicurean Philosophy: Revisiting Drive Theory," *Contemporary Psychoanalysis* 50, no. 3 (2014): 395-559, 396.

20   Bertrand Russell, *The Conquest of Happiness* (New York: W.W. Norton & Company Inc., 1996).

21   Blais Pascal, *Pensees*, trans. A. J. Krailsheimer (New York: Penguin Classics, 1995/1670).

22   Irvin Yalom, *Existential Psychotherapy* (New York: Basic Books, 1980), 483

23   Morris Berman, *Wandering God: A Study in Nomadic Spirituality* (Albany, NY: State University of New York Press, 2000), 46

24   Ernest Becker, *The Denial of Death* (New York: Free Press Paperbacks, 1997/1993), 68-69.

25   Pierre Teilhard de Chardin, *The Phenomenon of Man* (New York: Harper Collins, 2008), 165.

26   Ibid., 165.

27   Friedrich Nietzsche, *The Will to Power* (London: Allen, 1924).

28   Jonathan Yahalom, "Freud and Epicurean Philosophy: Revisiting Drive Theory," *Contemporary Psychoanalysis* 50, no. 3 (2014): 395-559.

29   Ernest Becker, *The Birth and Death of Meaning: An Interdisciplinary Perspective on the Problem of Man,* 2nd ed. (New York: The Free Press, 1972).

30   Leo Tolstoy, *My Confession, My Religion, The Gospel in Brief* (New York: Charles Scriber, 1929) 20.

31   Paul Wong, "Meaning-Centered Counselling," in *The Human Quest for Meaning: A Handbook of Psychological Research and Clinical Applications*, eds. Paul Wong and P.S. Fry (Mahwah, NJ: Erlbahm, 1998): 12.

32   Joseph Campbell, *Myths to Live By,* (New York: Penguin Compass, 1993).

33   Viktor Frankl, *The Will to Meaning* (New York: New American Library Inc, 1969).

34   Irvin Yalom, *Existential Psychotherapy* (New York: Basic Books, 1980).

35   Thomas Wartenberg, *Existentialism: A Beginner's Guide* (Oxford, England: Oneworld Publications, 2008).

36   Zvi Bellin, *Exploring a Holistic Content Approach to Personal Meaning* (Doctoral Thesis, 2009), Retrieved from http://meaningthoughbeing.com/

37   Lars Svendsen, *A Philosophy of Boredom*, trans. J. Irons (London: Reaktion Books, 2005).

38   Bruce Chatwin, *The Songlines* (New York: Penguin Books, 1988).

39   P. Norman et al., "The Evolutionary Mismatch Hypothesis: Implications for Psychological Science" *Current Directions in Psychological Science* 27 no. 1 (2018): 38-44.

40   Morris Berman, *Wandering God: A Study in Nomadic Spirituality* (Albany, NY: State University of New York Press, 2000).

41   Ibid., 16.

42   Ibid.

43   Jon Card, *Douglas Coupland: The 9-5 is Barbaric*: https://www.theguardian.com/small-business-network/2017/mar/30/douglas-coupland-the-nine-to-five-is-barbaric

44   Jose Ortega Y Gasset, *Meditations on Hunting* (New York: Scribner, 1972).

45   Morris Berman, *Wandering God: A Study in Nomadic Spirituality* (Albany, NY: State University of New York Press, 2000).

46   https://www.health.harvard.edu/mind-and-mood/endorphins-the-brains-natural-pain-reliever

47   Abraham Maslow, *Religion, Values, and Peak Experiences* (London: Penguin Books Limited, 1964).

48   Morris Berman, *Wandering God: A Study in Nomadic Spirituality* (Albany, NY: State University of New York Press, 2000).

49   Ibid.

50   Ibid.

51   Jose Ortega Y Gasset, *Meditations on Hunting* (New York: Scribner, 1972), 132-134.

52   Morris Berman, *Wandering God: A Study in Nomadic Spirituality* (Albany, NY: State University of New York Press, 2000).

53   Ibid., 138.

54   Jose Ortega Y Gasset, *Meditations on Hunting* (New York: Scribner, 1972), 132-134.

55   Ibid.

56   https://www.shiftelearning.com/blog/bid/350326/studies-confirm-the-power-of-visuals-in-elearning

57   Jose Ortega Y Gasset, *Meditations on Hunting* (New York: Scribner, 1972), 17.

58   Ed McGaa, *Nature's Way: Native Wisdom for Living in Balance with the Earth* (San Francisco: Harper Collins: 2004), 6.

59   Morris Berman, *Wandering God: A Study in Nomadic Spirituality* (Albany, NY: State University of New York Press, 2000).

60   Ibid.

61   Ibid.

62   James Suzman, *Affluence without Abundance: The Disappearing World of the Bushmen* (New York: Bloomsbury, 2017).

63   Morris Berman, *Wandering God: A Study in Nomadic Spirituality* (Albany, NY: State University of New York Press, 2000).

64   James Suzman, *Affluence without Abundance: The Disappearing World of the Bushmen* (New York: Bloomsbury, 2017).

65   Ibid.

66   Morris Berman, *Wandering God: A Study in Nomadic Spirituality* (Albany, NY: State University of New York Press, 2000),16.

67   Nathan Cofnas, "A Teleofunctional Account of Evolutionary Mismatch," *Journal of Biological Philosophy* 31 (2016): 507-525.

68   Morris Berman, *Wandering God: A Study in Nomadic Spirituality* (Albany, NY: State University of New York Press, 2000).

69   Ibid., 16.

70   James Suzman, *Affluence without Abundance: The Disappearing World of the Bushmen* (New York: Bloomsbury, 2017).

71   Lars Svendsen, *A Philosophy of Boredom*, trans. J. Irons (London: Reaktion Books, 2005).

72   Karl Jaspers, "The Axial Period," in Karl Jaspers, *The Origin and Goal of History* (New Haven: Yale University Press, 1953), 2.

73   Morris Berman, *Wandering God: A Study in Nomadic Spirituality* (Albany, NY: State University of New York Press, 2000).

74   Richard Tarnas, *Passion of the Western Mind: Understanding the Ideas That Have Shaped Our Worldview* (New York: Ballantine Books, 1993), 398.

75   Friedrich Nietzsche, *et al, The Gay Science* (Mineola, NY, Dover Publications Inc., 1882).

76   William James, *The Varieties of Religious Experience: A Study in Human Nature and Being* (New York: The Modern Library, 1994).

77   Richard Tarnas, *Passion of the Western Mind: Understanding the Ideas That Have Shaped Our Worldview* (New York: Ballantine Books, 1993), 370.

78   Zygmunt Bauman, *Liquid Modernity* (Cambridge, UK: Polity Press, 2015).

79   ———. "Education in Liquid Modernity *The Review of Education, Pedagogy, and Culture* 27 (2005): 303-317.

80   Ibid., 306.

81   ———. "Education in the Liquid Modern Setting *Power and Education* 1 No. 2 (2009): 157-156.

82   Andre Grace, *Lifelong Learning as Critical Action: International Perspectives on People, Politics, Policy and Practice*, (Toronto: Canadian Scholars Press Inc., 2013).

83   Todd May, *The Philosophy of Foucault* (Montreal: McGill-Queens University Press, 2006).

84   https://financialpost.com/commodities/energy/kinder-morgan-clarifies-embarrassing-oil-spill-benefits-comments

85   Ernest Becker, *The Birth and Death of Meaning: An Interdisciplinary Perspective on the Problem of Man*, 2nd ed. (New York: The Free Press, 1972).

86   Yuval Noah Harari, *Homo Deus: A Brief History of Tomorrow* (New York: Signa Books, 2017).

87   Thomas Wartenberg, *Existentialism* (Oxford: One World Publications, 2008).

88   Fernando Pessoa, *Book of Disquiet* (New York: A New Directions Book, 2017), 34.

89   Lars Svendsen, *A Philosophy of Boredom*, trans. J.Irons (London: Reaktion Books, 2005).

90   Vikor Frankl, *Man's Search for Meaning* (Boston: Beacon Press, 1963). 186-187.

91   James Hollis, *Finding Meaning in the Second Half of Life* (New York: Penguin Random House, 2005).

92   Morris Berman, *Wandering God: A Study in Nomadic Spirituality* (Albany, NY: State University of New York Press, 2000), 5.

93   Soren Kierkegaard, *The Concept of Dread*, trans. Walter Lowrie (Princeton: Princeton University Press, 1957/1844), 41.

94   Sheldon Solomon, *The Worm at the Core: On the Role of Death in Life* (New York: Random House: 2015).

95   Morris Berman, *Wandering God: A Study in Nomadic Spirituality* (Albany, NY: State University of New York Press, 2000), 226.

96   Ed McGaa, Nature's Way: *Native Wisdom for Living in Balance with the Earth* (San Francisco: Harper Collins: 2004).

97   Zygmunt Bauman, *The Trouble with Being Human These Days* (2012), retrieved from http://baumaninstitute.leeds.ac.uk/video

98   Ernest Becker, "The Heroics of Everyday Life: A Theorist of Death Confronts His Own End," (Psychology Today, April 1974): 78.

99   Martin Heidegger, *Being and Time*, trans. John Macquarrie and Edward Robinson (San Francisco: Harper, 1962).

100   Joseph Campbell, *Myths to Live By* (New York: Penguin Compass, 1993).

101   Ashley Woodward, "Camus and Nihilism" *Sophia* 4, no. 50, (2011): 543-559.

102   Albert Camus, *Lyrical and Critical Essays*, ed. Phillip Thody (New York: Vintage Books, 1970), 90.

103   Kirk Schneider, Rediscovery of Awe: *Splendor, Mystery, and The Fluid Center of Life.* (St. Paul, MN: Paragon House, 2004), 175.

104   ———. "Rediscovering Awe: A New Front in Humanistic Psychology, Psychotherapy, and Society. *The Handbook of Humanistic Psychology: Theory, Research, and Practice,* 42, no. 1 (2008): 73-82.

105   Ibid.

106   J. Carson, "The Sublime and Education," *The Journal of Aesthetic Education* 40, no. 1 (2006): 79-93.

107   Paul Tillich, *Systematic Theology Vol. 3* (Chicago: University of Chicago Press, 1963), 249.

108   Albert Camus, *The Myth of Sisyphus and Other Essays* (New York: Vintage Books: 2000).

109   Albert Camus & J. O'Brien, *Resistance, rebellion, and death* (New York: Vintage International, 1995).

110   Albert Camus, *The Rebel* (New York: Vintage Books, 1991/1955), 255.

111   Ibid., 70.

112   Albert Camus, *The Myth of Sisyphus and Other Essays* (New York: Vintage Books: 2000), 68.

113   Epicurus, *The Essential Epicurus: Letters, Principal Doctrines, Vatican Sayings, and Fragments.* trans. E. M. O' Connor (Buffalo, NY: Prometheus Books, 1993), 66.

114   John Cooper, Pursuits of Wisdom: *Six Ways of Life in Ancient Philosophy from Socrates to Plotinus* (Princeton, NJ: Princeton University Press, 2012)

115   Ibid., 71

116   Albert Camus, *The Plague* (Harmondsworth, Middlesex, England: Penguin Books, 1973), 252

117   Ibid., 251-252.

118   Morris Berman, *Wandering God: A Study in Nomadic Spirituality* (Albany, NY: State University of New York Press, 2000), 244.

MARK A. HAWKINS, PH.D., is an author, educator, and a clinical counsellor. His research focuses on interdisciplinary understandings of meaning and purpose as they relate to human wellbeing. He is the author of *The Power of Boredom: Why Boredom is Essential for Creating a Meaningful Life.*

Manufactured by Amazon.ca
Bolton, ON

31581611R00092